HOW TO UNDERSTAND YOURSELF AND OTHERS

USING THE ENNEAGRAM TO DISCOVER YOUR TRUE SELF AND BUILD RELATIONSHIPS

KIM PRYOR JONES

CANTONFIELD PUBLISHING

CONTENTS

CHAPTER 1
READY TO BEGIN THE JOURNEY?

Have you ever felt like you just don't quite understand yourself or the people around you? Like there's some secret to who you are and how you connect with others that you just can't seem to uncover? Well, my friend, you've come to the right place. This book is going to take you on a journey of self-discovery and relationship building using a fascinating tool called the Enneagram.

Now, unless you've done some digging already, you're probably wondering what on earth the Enneagram even is! Don't worry, I'll give you the lowdown. The Enneagram is an ancient system that describes 9 different personality types that people identify with. These types are based on our core motivations, fears, and desires. Pretty cool, right?

By figuring out your Enneagram type, you'll gain access to a wealth of insights about yourself. It's like finding the missing puzzle piece to understanding why you think, act, and feel the way you do. Suddenly, so many things will start to make sense!

But the Enneagram doesn't just stop at describing your personality. It also maps out the journey of growth for each type. This means you'll get to see how to overcome your weaknesses and limitations to become the best and healthiest version of yourself. Now we're talking!

And if that wasn't enough, the Enneagram also shines a light on how you interact with other personality types. This information is pure gold when it comes to building strong, lasting relationships in all areas of your life. You'll learn how to identify other people's types, what motivates them, and how to communicate effectively with them based on their core desires and fears. Your relationships will never be the same again!

So by now, I hope you're getting excited about how the Enneagram can be a total game changer in your life. But I bet you still have a ton of questions like:

How do I figure out my Enneagram type? What are the 9 types and what are they like? Can someone have traits of multiple types? How does this help me reach my potential? Can the Enneagram improve my relationships? How do I use the Enneagram to understand others better?

Don't worry, this book will answer all those burning questions and more! I'll explain everything in a super friendly and simple way - no prior knowledge of the

Enneagram necessary. We'll start from square one together.

Here's a quick sneak peek of what we'll get up to in just the first few chapters:

In Chapter 1, we'll do a quick history lesson and learn all about the origins and development of the Enneagram over the centuries. I know history isn't everyone's favorite subject, but trust me, this is fascinating stuff!

Chapter 2 is where we'll really get into the nitty gritty of what the heck the 9 Enneagram types actually are. The special traits, core motivations and common behaviors of each type will be described so you can start getting a feel for them.

Chapter 3 is the fun part where you get to do some self-reflection and take a crack at figuring out your own Enneagram type! I'll explain the different methods you can use to accurately type yourself, because yes, there is a right way and a wrong way to do it.

In Chapter 4, we'll explore the unique dynamics between the types when they interact with each other. You'll learn how to spot each type, communicate effectively with them, and avoid common conflicts based on their motivations. Get ready for those quality relationships!

Chapter 5 focuses on personal growth, which is what the Enneagram is ultimately all about. I'll explain how to leverage your type's strengths as well as overcome the limitations holding you back from your full potential. You'll be unstoppable!

Chapter 6 homed in on using your Enneagram insights to improve your relationships. You'll learn how to resolve conflict, enhance intimacy, support each other's growth, and create a cherished union.

In Chapter 7, we'll discuss how to apply the Enneagram at work to skyrocket your professional development and create an awesome team culture. Yes, it's just as useful at work as in your personal life!

Finally, Chapter 8 will cover some key ethical guidelines in using the Enneagram so that you avoid misusing this powerful tool. I don't want you getting into any tricky situations because you didn't know any better!

Whew, was that a mouthful or what? As you can see, this book will cover everything you need and more to truly harness the gifts of the Enneagram. I don't want to over-whelm you, so let's just take it one step at a time together.

Each chapter ends with a handy summary so you can review the key points. I encourage you to take some time to let the concepts and insights digest so you can inte-grate them fully. A few reflection questions are also there for you to check your understanding.

My goal is that by the end of this book, you'll feel like you've made a new best friend in the Enneagram that will support you for life. With your new Enneagram wisdom, you'll understand on a whole new level what makes you and others tick. Your confidence, compassion, and connections will skyrocket. You'll feel empowered to grow, give, and live with purpose.

So, are you ready for the adventure of a lifetime? I'm so pumped to take this journey with you and watch you blossom into your highest potential. Let's get going, my friend! There's so much exciting stuff to uncover about yourself and others. Your transformation begins now!

CHAPTER 2
HISTORY AND OVERVIEW OF THE ENNEAGRAM

Ready to explore the captivating world of the Enneagram! This chapter uncovers its rich history and the Enneagram's nine personality types. Exploring these nine types, you'll find a compass for personal growth and building meaningful relationships. The Enneagram isn't just a tool for understanding others; it's a gateway to understanding yourself better. So, brace yourself for an exciting self-discovery journey, and let the Enneagram illuminate your path to self-improvement and service to others.

ORIGINS OF THE ENNEAGRAM

The Enneagram system, utilized since ancient times by diverse cultures and spiritual traditions, is thought to have originated in the Middle East, with potential roots in Sufi teachings or early Christian mysticism. The fourth-century Christian monk Evagrius Ponticus mentioned the Enneagram in his writings, aligning nine fundamental human vices with the system's nine personality types, suggesting it's been used for self-improvement for centuries.

In the 20th century, Bolivian philosopher Oscar Ichazo introduced the Enneagram to the West, combining psychological and spiritual insights to understand human behavior. Since then, numerous scholars have expanded and popularized the Enneagram, making it a valuable tool in fields like psychology, counseling, leadership development, and relationship dynamics.

KEY FIGURES IN ENNEAGRAM DEVELOPMENT

Now, let's explore the key figures who played a crucial role in the development of the Enneagram system. These pioneers, influential contributors, and foundational figures have provided valuable insights into the various aspects of the Enneagram. By studying their work and understanding their perspectives, you can gain a deeper understanding of this powerful tool for self-awareness and personal growth.

Enneagram Pioneers

Oscar Ichazo, a key figure in the development of the Enneagram system, brought the Enneagram of Personality to the Western world in the 1970s, establishing the basis for understanding the nine unique personality types and their interconnection. Several other contributors significantly enhanced the system's growth and popularity: Claudio Naranjo merged the Enneagram system with psychology, extending its application in therapy and personal growth. Helen Palmer popularized the Enneagram through her writings and teachings. Don Richard Riso and Russ Hudson founded the Enneagram Institute and wrote key books explaining the nine types and their motivations. Beatrice Chestnut's work focused on the Enneagram's potential for transformation and self-awareness. Their collective efforts have assisted many in their personal growth and comprehension journeys.

Influential Contributors

Key contributors to the development of the Enneagram system include Oscar Ichazo, who introduced it to the Western world in the 1960s, laying the groundwork for understanding the nine personality types. Claudio Naranjo expanded on Ichazo's work, integrating psychology into the system and deepening its application in personal growth and self-awareness. Don Riso and Russ Hudson further popularized the Enneagram through their research, books, and workshops, contributing significantly to its evolution and potential for transformation. These individuals have enriched our understanding of ourselves and others, fostering compassion and empathy.

Foundational Figure Insights

Discussing the Enneagram system's Foundational Figure Insights, let's explore the perspectives and contributions of four key figures.

1. **Gurdjieff and Ouspensky:** They advocated for self-awareness and an integrated approach to personal growth, encompassing body, mind, and emotions.
2. **Ichazo and Naranjo:** They introduced the nine unique personality types, underlining the need for self-reflection and transformation.
3. **Riso and Hudson:** Their research identified core motivations and fears of each type, assisting in self-discovery and development.
4. **Palmer and Daniels:** They concentrated on the Enneagram's spiritual aspects, guiding towards self-acceptance, compassion, and spiritual growth.

Understanding these figures and their insights can enhance your ability to help others on their journey to self-awareness and transformation through the Enneagram system.

THE ENNEAGRAM AS A PERSONALITY SYSTEM

Exploring the Enneagram personality system offers deep insight into human nature beyond the mere categorization of nine types. It not only helps to understand one's motivations, fears, and behavior patterns but also enhances personal growth and self-awareness. Identifying your primary Enneagram type enables you to comprehend your strengths, weaknesses, and thought processes, paving the way for better decision-making and self-alignment.

Moreover, the Enneagram system also fosters improved relationships. By understanding the Enneagram types of others, empathy and appreciation for their viewpoints increase, and communication becomes more effective. Recognizing potential triggers in interactions can aid in conflict resolution.

The Enneagram offers a development roadmap for each type, highlighting areas for growth and aiding in reaching full potential. This integration can lead to increased compassion, self-awareness, and authenticity.

NINE TYPES OF THE ENNEAGRAM

The Enneagram personality system helps you identify your primary type, offering insight into your motivations, fears, and behaviors. It classifies people into nine unique types.

1. Type One - The Perfectionist: You aim for perfection, driven by a strong moral compass. Your desire to better the world inspires others.
2. Type Two - The Helper: You're empathetic, always willing to assist. Your ability to foresee others' needs allows you to offer support.
3. Type Three - The Achiever: You're ambitious, seeking success and recognition. Your determination motivates others to reach their goals.

4. Type Four - The Individualist: You're sensitive and creative, craving authenticity. Your emotional expressiveness encourages others to be unique.
5. Type Five - The Investigator: You are a curious, insightful thinker who enjoys learning and acquiring knowledge. Your inquisitive nature leads others to question and explore.
6. Type Six - The Loyalist: You value security and support, often putting others' needs before your own. Your loyalty and reliability are comforting to those around you.
7. Type Seven - The Enthusiast: You are an energetic, optimistic individual who enjoys new experiences. Your enthusiasm inspires others to seek joy and adventure.
8. Type Eight - The Challenger: You are a strong, confident leader who protects those you care about. Your assertiveness encourages others to stand up for their beliefs.
9. Type Nine - The Peacemaker: You are a calm, accepting individual who seeks harmony. Your peaceful demeanor encourages others to resolve conflicts and maintain balance.

Understanding these types equips you to appreciate diverse personalities and viewpoints, fostering compassion and empathy in your interactions. The Enneagram isn't about labeling but promoting personal growth and building strong relationships.

UNDERSTANDING THE ENNEAGRAM TRIADS

Continuing our discussion on the Enneagram system, we now explore the Enneagram Triads, a crucial component providing insights into our emotional, cognitive, and instinctual influences.

The Triads comprise the Gut, Heart, and Head groups, each incorporating three Enneagram types with shared behavioral patterns.

The Gut Triad includes Types 8, 9, and 1, marked by instinctual reactions and a reliance on gut feelings. These people value control, justice, and integrity and often grapple with anger and control issues.

The Heart Triad consists of Types 2, 3, and 4, focused on emotions, validation, and connection. These individuals' drive is their feelings and the longing for acceptance, often struggling with self-image, identity, and external validation.

The Head Triad encompasses Types 5, 6, and 7, who are rooted in their thoughts and ideas. They rely on their intellect, often over-analyzing situations, and frequently deal with fear, anxiety, and uncertainty.

Understanding the Enneagram Triads helps identify behavioral, emotional, and cognitive patterns. Recognizing our Triad can provide insights into our strengths, weaknesses, and growth areas, fostering self-understanding, compassion, empathy, and better service to others.

ENNEAGRAM WINGS AND INTEGRATION/DISINTEGRATION

Diving into Enneagram Wings and their part in integration/disintegration can offer several benefits.

1. **Growth:** Your Enneagram wing can significantly aid your personal development. By understanding your wing, you can identify your strengths and areas needing improvement, thereby fostering growth.

2. **Integration:** The wing can act as a connector between your core type and another type's qualities. Integrating your wing introduces you to positive attributes of that type, boosting your well-being and efficiency. This process promotes balance and personal integration.

3. **Disintegration:** Conversely, disintegration can amplify your core type's negative aspects. Your wing can heighten fears, anxieties, and unhealthy habits. Understanding your wing's influence during stressful times can aid self-awareness and self-correction.

4. **Self-understanding:** Comprehending your Enneagram wing enhances self-compassion and understanding. It highlights your dynamic, multifaceted personality and your ability to access various qualities and strengths. Use your wing for personal growth and transformation.

Exploring Enneagram Wings and their role in integration and disintegration deepens self-understanding and empathy towards others. This knowledge can empower you to serve others compassionately and boost personal growth. Harness your Enneagram wing for self-discovery and transformation.

MODERN APPLICATIONS OF THE ENNEAGRAM

The Enneagram's modern applications can facilitate personal growth and enhance relationships. Its insights into our motivations and fears are used in various fields for personal development, leadership, and interpersonal dynamics.

For personal growth, the Enneagram serves as a guide for self-discovery and self-awareness, helping identify behavioral patterns and areas for improvement. It helps overcome self-limiting beliefs, manage stress, and foster healthy habits, offering a personalized framework for development.

In leadership, the Enneagram aids in understanding how individuals respond to challenges and interact, enabling the adaptation of leadership styles to meet team needs, resulting in better communication, increased motivation, and a harmonious work environment.

The Enneagram also improves relationships by fostering empathy and understanding, leading to compassionate and effective communication, and subsequently, stronger connections.

CRITICISMS AND CONTROVERSIES SURROUNDING THE ENNEAGRAM

Enneagram, a popular self-improvement tool, faces criticisms and controversies regarding its validity and scientific basis. Four main criticisms include:

1. Lack of scientific evidence: Critics question its psychological basis and reliance on subjective interpretations and anecdotal evidence.
2. Overgeneralization and stereotyping: Skeptics argue that the Enneagram's personality categorization is overly simplistic and fails to account for individual human behavior complexities.
3. Lack of standardization: The inconsistency across different schools and practitioners raises concerns about its accuracy and validity.
4. Commercialization and commodification: High-priced workshops, certifications, and merchandise have led to concerns about the credibility and authenticity of the Enneagram.

Despite these criticisms, many individuals value the Enneagram for its insights and help in personal growth. The decision to use it as a self-discovery tool rests with the individual.

FREQUENTLY ASKED QUESTIONS

How Can I Use the Enneagram to Improve My Relationships?

Looking to boost your relationships with the Enneagram? Start by getting a handle on your own type and what drives you. Next, dive into learning about the types of those around you. This can help you understand their needs and actions. With this info, you can communicate more effectively, show empathy, and give the right kind of support. Spot any behavior patterns that might stir up trouble and tackle them head-on. And always remember, everyone's unique - so make sure compassion and understanding are at the heart of your relationships.

Are There Any Famous Individuals or Celebrities Who Have Publicly Identified With a Specific Enneagram Type?

Absolutely! Famous personalities like Oprah Winfrey, Barack Obama, and Lady Gaga have openly shared their enneagram types. Oprah is a Type 3 - The Achiever, Obama is a Type 9 - The Peacemaker, and Lady Gaga is a Type 4 - The Individualist. This sharing gives us a peek into their personalities and what drives them. By knowing their enneagram types, you can understand them better and even find some insights about your own type. So, dive in and explore!

Can the Enneagram Be Used as a Tool for Personal Growth and Self-Improvement?

Sure, the Enneagram can definitely be your guide to personal growth and self-improvement! When you understand your Enneagram type, you unlock a deeper understanding of your core motivations, fears, and desires. It's like having a map to your inner self. You'll see patterns and behaviors that might be slowing you down. And guess what? You can use that knowledge to build healthier habits and make positive changes. The Enneagram can be a strong tool in your personal growth toolbox, steering you towards a life that's more fulfilling and authentic. So, why wait? Start your journey now!

Is There a Specific Age Range or Demographic That the Enneagram Is Most Applicable To?

The Enneagram works for all, no matter how old you are or where you come from. Think of it as your personal guide to understanding yourself better. It doesn't matter if you're young, old, a man, or a woman. The Enneagram gives you a peek into your personality and how you behave. It uncovers what you're good at and where you need to improve. So, don't box yourself in because of age or where you come from - the Enneagram is here for everyone. Make that change and live a happier life!

Are There Any Scientific Studies or Research That Validate the Accuracy and Effectiveness of the Enneagram System?

Looking for scientific proof backing the enneagram system's accuracy and effectiveness? You're in luck! There have been studies conducted that delve into its reliability and validity. Many of these studies show promising results. Although more research is still on the horizon, the current studies hint at the enneagram being a valuable tool for self-awareness and personal growth. So, go ahead, dive into the world of the enneagram and discover its potential benefits with confidence!

CONCLUSION

Dive right into the fascinating chapter of the Enneagram system's history. It's a complex yet captivating mix of personalities and motivations. With nine types, triads, and wings, the Enneagram gives us a unique peek into human behavior and personal growth. Its journey from distant past to today is quite a story, with plenty of fans and critics along the way. So, prepare to unveil the complexities and discover what they can reveal about your inner self.

CHAPTER 3

WHAT ARE THE 9 ENNEAGRAM TYPES?

Interested in the 9 Enneagram types? Want to get a better understanding of yourself and others? You've come to the right place! This chapter provides detailed descriptions and real-life examples of each type: the Perfectionist, the Helper, the Achiever, the Individualist, the Investigator, the Loyalist, the Enthusiast, the Challenger, and the Peacemaker. Buckle up for an exciting journey of self-discovery and insights to enrich your life!

ENNEAGRAM TYPE 1: THE PERFECTIONIST

As an Enneagram Type 1, The Perfectionist, your meticulousness and high standards fuel your pursuit of excellence. Your innate desire to serve others and make a positive impact is driven by your strong sense of responsibility. Your unparalleled attention to detail and ability to spot errors enable you to produce high-quality work, regardless of the setting. Your approach involves careful analysis and precision in every task.

However, these high standards can lead to self-criticism and feelings of inadequacy. Despite this, your pursuit of excellence and attention to detail make you an indispensable asset to any team or organization. Your commitment to serving others is evident in your dedication to delivering outstanding results. As a Perfectionist, your meticulousness and desire to serve make you valuable, and while your high standards can be challenging, they enhance your ability to positively impact others' lives.

ENNEAGRAM TYPE 2: THE HELPER

As an Enneagram Type 2, The Helper, you have a strong inclination to support and care for others. Your innate nurturing qualities enable you to connect deeply with people, understanding their needs and emotions. Your life reflects your desire to serve others, finding joy and purpose in assisting those in need. Your empathetic nature allows you to anticipate others' needs, providing comfort and support. However, it's vital to establish boundaries and prioritize self-care as you might tend to neglect your own needs. In relationships, your selflessness strengthens deep connections and lasting bonds. As a summary, your genuine desire to help, coupled with your nurturing and empathetic nature, makes you invaluable to those around you, but remember to care for yourself too.

ENNEAGRAM TYPE 3: THE ACHIEVER

Type 3 of the Enneagram, The Achiever, is characterized by a focus on success, recognition, and the desire to excel. As an Achiever, you're driven, goal-oriented, and possess a natural talent for influencing others through your charm and charisma. These traits can lead to success in various fields such as business, politics, and entertainment.

You flourish in situations where you can display your skills and achievements, underpinned by your dedication, hard work, and high personal standards. Your ambition stems from a deep-seated need for validation and praise.

However, this drive can lead to prioritizing external validation over self-care and authenticity. Balance between the desire for achievement and the need for self-care and genuine relationships is critical.

ENNEAGRAM TYPE 4: THE INDIVIDUALIST

As an Individualist, you possess unique characteristics and motivations that set you apart from others. Your creative expression is a powerful outlet for your complex emotions, allowing you to explore and express your inner world in a way that is both authentic and deeply personal. Understanding these points will help you navigate your journey of self-discovery and embrace your individuality with confidence.

Unique Characteristics and Motivations

Enneagram Type 4s are distinguished by their deep individuality and self-expression. They crave recognition for their uniqueness and tend to express their deepest feelings and thoughts. As highly creative, original, and authentic individuals, Type 4s often introspect, exploring their emotions and seeking life's deeper meaning. They are driven by a need to be understood and acknowledged for their individuality. Their desire to serve others comes through their unique perspectives and creative insights, helping others appreciate their own individuality.

Creative Expression and Emotions

As an Enneagram Type 4, the Individualist, use your unique ability to express emotions creatively. Your artistic nature enables deep connections with others, offering solace and understanding. Through mediums like painting, writing, or music, your creativity can uplift others. Harness your sensitivity to produce art that touches people's hearts. Sharing your genuine emotions creates a safe space for others to explore theirs. Your creative pursuits can inspire and heal, serving others in a significant and impactful manner.

ENNEAGRAM TYPE 5: THE INVESTIGATOR

As a Type 5, you have a fear of being overwhelmed by the demands of the world, which drives your need for knowledge and understanding. You are naturally analytical and observant, always seeking to gather information and make sense of the world around you. Your inquisitive nature allows you to delve deep into complex subjects, making you a valuable source of expertise in your chosen field.

Fear of Being Overwhelmed

If you're an Enneagram Type 5, or The Investigator, you may grapple with the fear of being overwhelmed due to your profound need for knowledge and understanding. This fear, often triggered by your instinct to amass and scrutinize information, may cause you to seek solitude and privacy. It's crucial to manage this fear to efficiently serve others and maintain your well-being. To do this, set boundaries, prioritize self-care, and delegate tasks when needed. Remember, it's okay to seek help and take breaks when required. By managing your fear of being overwhelmed, you can continue to help others while preserving your own well-being.

Analytical and Observant

Enneagram Type 5, The Investigator, is known for their analytical and observant traits. Their methodical approach to acquiring knowledge involves extensive research and a desire to become experts in their chosen fields. They are adept at analysis, often spotting patterns and connections missed by others. Their keen observational skills enable them to notice minute details, helping them see the larger context. Understanding and leveraging these qualities can enhance partnership with The

Investigator, allowing their unique insights and expertise to benefit others.

Desire for Knowledge

The Investigator's quest for knowledge compels comprehensive research in your chosen field, leading to expertise. Your unquenchable curiosity and need for understanding the world's complexities drive your pursuit of truth and knowledge expansion. Your thoroughness ensures no detail is overlooked, excelling in data analysis and insight synthesis. This passion for knowledge benefits you and others by sharing your expertise and offering valuable guidance.

ENNEAGRAM TYPE 6: THE LOYALIST

Enneagram Type 6, The Loyalist, is characterized by a strong commitment and a tendency to anticipate potential threats, making them reliable and protective. Key traits include:

- **Commitment:** They're dedicated, reliable, and fulfill their obligations, making them trustworthy allies.
- **Anticipating Threats:** They're often consumed by worry and actively scan their surroundings for threats to protect themselves and others.

Understanding their subtypes can aid in supporting Type 6 individuals:

1. **Phobic Loyalist:** They're typically more anxious, dependent on reassurance, and align with trusted authorities for safety.
2. **Counterphobic Loyalist:** They confront fears directly, showing a rebellious attitude and a desire to overcome anxieties.

Creating a safe, reassuring, valuable environment, providing dependable guidance, and offering personal growth opportunities can enhance their loyalty and dedication.

ENNEAGRAM TYPE 7: THE ENTHUSIAST

Enneagram Type 7, The Enthusiast, is characterized by an adventurous spirit, a craving for variety, and an inherent curiosity for new experiences. This type is always looking for ways to broaden their perspective and find joy in their surroundings.

Enthusiasts spread positivity and lift others' spirits with their infectious energy, making them ideal companions for adventure seekers. However, their constant quest for diversity can lead to restlessness and a fear of missing out, often struggling to commit to a single path or project.

To serve others effectively, Enthusiasts should develop balance and discipline. Their enthusiasm is a notable strength, but it's crucial to also value stability and commitment. Grounding themselves and maintaining focus will enhance their reliability, benefiting those around them.

ENNEAGRAM TYPE 8: THE CHALLENGER

As an Enneagram Type 8, The Challenger, you are assertive, driven, and a natural leader who aims to positively impact the world. Your determination motivates others to act and support their beliefs. Key characteristics of Type 8 include:

- **Assertiveness**: You're confident and unafraid to express your opinions, which can be seen as admirable or intimidating.
- **Drive for Control**: You crave autonomy and self-reliance, avoiding dependency.
- *Leadership*: Your inherent leadership skills enable you to guide others in achieving their goals.
- *Protector*: Your strong justice and fairness instincts lead you to safeguard those who can't protect themselves.

While your assertiveness and control drive can be assets, they can also be overwhelming to others. Balancing your strong personality with empathy and active listening can foster a supportive environment where everyone feels valued. True strength lies in empowering others, not just in asserting your own needs.

ENNEAGRAM TYPE 9: THE PEACEMAKER

Enneagram Type 9, The Peacemaker, prioritizes harmony, often putting others' needs before their own to avoid conflict. They have a unique ability to mediate disputes and foster unity due to their empathetic nature and calming presence. However, this desire for peace can lead to self-neglect, as they might suppress personal desires and opinions to maintain tranquility. Their fear of upsetting others can cause indecisiveness, inertia, and a tendency to follow others' plans without advocating for themselves. To assist a Peacemaker, it's crucial to provide a secure, non-judgmental space for them to express themselves and encourage them to voice their needs. Reassuring them can alleviate their fear of conflict and help them assert themselves confidently. In essence, Peacemakers have a strong inclination towards harmony but may struggle with self-assertion. By creating a supportive environment, we can help them find their voice, contributing to a more balanced and peaceful world.

FREQUENTLY ASKED QUESTIONS

How Can I Determine My Enneagram Type?

Want to find out your Enneagram type? Dive deep into your motivations and habits. Think about what scares you, what you want, and what you believe in. Notice how you respond in various situations and the patterns in how you act. You might find it helpful to chat with an

Enneagram expert or take an online test to get a head start. Remember, the Enneagram is all about uncovering more about yourself and growing as a person, so embrace the journey of self-discovery.

Can a Person Have Traits From Multiple Enneagram Types?

Absolutely! You can definitely show traits from several enneagram types. Everyone is unique, and it's normal to display features from various types. The enneagram is there to help you get to know yourself, not to limit you to one particular category. Embrace your personality's diversity and see which types you connect with. Keep in mind, the enneagram is all about self-discovery, and it's perfectly fine to exhibit traits from more than one type.

Are There Any Famous Individuals Who Embody Each Enneagram Type?

Ever wondered if any celebrities align with each enneagram type? Good news - they do! All types, from the perfectionist to the achiever, and the helper to the individualist, are represented among the stars. If you're keen to understand the link between personality types and fame, it's time to jump into the exciting world of the enneagram. Let's discover which famous faces fit each type!

Can Someone's Enneagram Type Change Over Time?

Sure, your Enneagram type can change as you grow! Remember, the Enneagram isn't set in stone; you can evolve. As you become more self-aware and focus on personal growth, your Enneagram type might shift. This doesn't mean you're changing at your core, but that you're becoming more balanced, more integrated. So, go ahead, embrace this journey of self-discovery and let yourself evolve into the best version of you!

What Are Some Common Misconceptions About the Enneagram Types?

Let's chat about some common myths about Enneagram types, shall we? You may believe that a person's type is their entire identity, but that's not really the case. Each type is more than just a label. Also, you might think you can only possess traits from one type, but we're all a blend of different traits. By clearing up these misconceptions, you can start to see the Enneagram as a tool for personal growth and self-awareness, rather than a strict box to fit into. So, embrace the diversity of your traits and use them to flourish!

CONCLUSION

Imagine each type as a different chapter in a book. There's the Perfectionist, always chasing flawlessness, and the Peacemaker, who seeks harmony and inner peace, among others. This isn't just some dry theory, but a vibrant kaleidoscope that shows us the stunning diversity of human personalities. It's all about understanding and celebrating our differences while pushing ourselves to reach our fullest potential.

CHAPTER 4
CORE MOTIVATIONS AND FEARS

Ever catch yourself in a constant hustle for perfection? Or do you simply love lending a helping hand, making a world of difference in other people's lives? Or maybe, you're the type who's fueled by success, constantly pushing your limits to stay ahead. Whichever path you're on, the Enneagram is a handy tool for understanding what really drives you and what you fear the most. In this chapter, we're going to delve into the world of the 9 Enneagram types and how they influence our dreams and goals. Brace yourself, as we're about to dig deep into your true self and uncover ways to lead a more contented life.

ENNEAGRAM TYPE 1: THE PERFECTIONIST

As an Enneagram Type 1, or The Perfectionist, your driving force is achieving perfection to avoid criticism and uphold integrity. You naturally desire to serve others and improve the world, believing perfection in your actions contributes to the greater good.

Your meticulous nature and high standards extend to yourself and others, fueling your pursuit to rectify perceived flaws or injustices. This devotion to excellence and positive change points to your service to others.

However, this relentless quest for perfection can be daunting, leading to self-criticism and feelings of frustration and doubt. It's vital to remember that perfection is unattainable and mistakes are part of growth.

Balancing self-compassion and self-care with your pursuit for excellence is essential. Realize that serving others includes self-care and rest. By maintaining a balance between striving for excellence and self-acceptance, you can continue to positively impact the world while preserving your well-being.

ENNEAGRAM TYPE 2: THE HELPER

Let's talk about the Helper, also known as Enneagram Type 2. The Helper's core motivation is to be loved and needed by others, often going above and beyond to meet their needs. However, their biggest fear is being rejected or unwanted, which can drive them to constantly seek validation and approval from others.

Helper's Core Motivation

As an Enneagram Type 2, or the Helper, your core motivation revolves around the need to feel valued and essential to others. You are driven by the following:

1. **Indispensability**: You want to be seen as vital in the lives of those around you, fearing insignificance.
2. **Validation**: You seek affirmation for your selfless efforts, which gives you a sense of purpose and satisfaction.
3. **Relationship Building**: Your motivation centers around forming meaningful connections and fostering a sense of unity in your community.

Understanding these motivations can guide you to positively impact others while addressing your own needs.

Helper's Biggest Fear?

The Helper's main fear is rejection and feeling unloved or unappreciated. As a Helper, their deep-seated need to serve others can lead to self-neglect and overextending oneself due to a fear of abandonment. Constantly seeking validation can occur, but it's crucial to realize that worth isn't determined by how much one does for others. Practicing self-care and setting boundaries can help mitigate these fears, allowing Helpers to serve authentically.

ENNEAGRAM TYPE 3: THE ACHIEVER

You are an Enneagram Type 3, also known as The Achiever. Your core motivation is driven by a desire for success and recognition. You excel at balancing ambition and authenticity, constantly striving to achieve your goals while also staying true to yourself.

Success-Driven Personality Traits

Enneagram Type 3, The Achiever, is characterized by a relentless drive for achievement and recognition. They're motivated by setting and achieving ambitious goals, always aiming for excellence. Key traits include:

1. **Ambition**: They constantly seek new challenges and growth opportunities, setting high standards and pushing themselves to reach their potential.
2. **Competitiveness**: They thrive on competition and being seen as the best, driven to outperform others and validate their worth through their achievements.
3. **Desire for Validation**: They seek external approval and thrive on praise for their accomplishments, reinforcing their self-worth and boosting confidence.

Understanding these traits can help support and motivate The Achiever to reach their goals and positively impact others.

Balancing Ambition and Authenticity

Enneagram Type 3 individuals, or Achievers, need to balance their ambition for success with authentic self-expression. These highly motivated individuals often strive for recognition, but this can sometimes overshadow their true selves, leading to a loss of authenticity. To maintain authenticity, Achievers should reflect on their values and personal growth, align their ambitions with their true desires, and serve others in a meaningful way. This allows them to achieve success while remaining true to themselves.

ENNEAGRAM TYPE 4: THE INDIVIDUALIST

Enneagram Type 4, or the Individualist, is driven by a desire for uniqueness and a fear of being common. As an Individualist, you seek to express your authentic self and be acknowledged for your distinct traits. However, you also fear being seen as mundane and strive to maintain your individuality.

To understand the Individualist's motivations and fears, consider these points:

1. **Desire for self-expression:** You yearn to express your emotions, thoughts, and creativity authentically. This need arises from your longing for authenticity and desire to be seen and understood for your unique viewpoint.
2. **Quest for significance:** You aim to create a meaningful life and seek experiences and relationships that make you feel valued. This

drive is fueled by a fear of being ignored or forgotten.

3. **Fear of being ordinary:** You dread being average or ordinary, associating it with being insignificant or unloved. To overcome this fear, you often seek unique paths and reject societal norms.

Recognizing your core motivation and fear as an Individualist can guide you towards self-discovery and authenticity. By accepting your unique traits and finding appropriate ways to express yourself, you can achieve fulfillment and create a life that aligns with your deepest desires.

ENNEAGRAM TYPE 5: THE INVESTIGATOR

As an Enneagram Type 5 Investigator, you're motivated by a deep-seated desire for knowledge and expertise across various domains. This curiosity propels your exploration of intricate ideas and concepts. You aim to utilize your knowledge to assist others, providing valuable insights and solutions through your analytical thinking and research skills.

However, be aware of your propensity to retreat from social interactions due to fears of being overwhelmed. It's crucial to couple your intellectual contributions with emotional connections and relationship building.

Fields requiring critical thinking, analysis, and problem-solving suit your meticulous attention to detail and pattern recognition abilities, making you a key player in research, academia, or any knowledge-driven profession.

ENNEAGRAM TYPE 6: THE LOYALIST

As an Enneagram Type 6 Loyalist, your primary drive is a longing for security and fear of uncertainty. You appreciate having a reliable support system and often need others' validation due to self-doubt.

Three defining traits of a Loyalist are:

1. **Loyalty and Commitment:** You highly value loyalty and are deeply committed to all relationships in your life, expecting the same in return.
2. **Seeking Security:** You seek stability, with uncertainty causing anxiety. You work hard to create a safe environment, often through planning, advice from trusted sources, or following established rules.
3. **Questioning and Doubt:** Fear of uncertainty leads to questioning and anticipating problems, sometimes resulting in overthinking. Trusting your judgment and abilities is a crucial growth step.

As a Loyalist, your wish to support others stems from your need for security. Being dependable enhances stability and trust. However, balancing the pursuit of security with accepting uncertainty is key to your growth.

ENNEAGRAM TYPE 7: THE ENTHUSIAST

Enneagram Type 7, or The Enthusiast, is driven by a thirst for experiences and a fear of missing out. As an Enthusiast, you are drawn to excitement and novelty, with a core motivation to avoid feeling confined. You aim to maximize life's potential, often finding yourself managing multiple ventures to satisfy your need for diversity and stimulation. However, this relentless quest can sometimes result in a lack of focus or commitment, causing you to bounce between activities without fully engaging in any.

Your desire to serve others equips you to bring energy and enthusiasm to any situation. Your excitement is infectious, boosting the spirits of those around you. Despite this, your continuous chase for new experiences can overwhelm others or make them feel neglected. It's crucial to invest time in deepening connections with others and being present in their lives.

As an Enthusiast, your goal is to savor all life offers, fueled by a fear of missing out. Your passion for life is infectious, and you naturally spread joy and excitement. However, remember to balance your pursuit of new experiences with the need to fully engage in the present and deepen your relationships.

ENNEAGRAM TYPE 8: THE CHALLENGER

Enneagram Type 8, known as the Challenger, is driven by a need for power and a fear of control. This type's key characteristics include a desire for control, fear of weakness, and a need for justice.

1. Challengers seek control over their surroundings and people, stemming from their need for autonomy and a fear of vulnerability. They naturally gravitate towards leadership and exert their power for self-protection.
2. They abhor showing weakness or vulnerability, always striving to appear strong, even when facing internal struggles.
3. Challengers have a strong sense of justice, standing against oppression and injustice. They are driven to protect the underdog and fight against perceived unfair authority, fueled by their fear of being controlled.

Understanding these motivations and fears of the Challenger can foster better connections with individuals of this type, by addressing their need for control, fear of appearing weak, and their quest for justice with empathy and compassion.

ENNEAGRAM TYPE 9: THE PEACEMAKER

Enneagram Type 9, the Peacemaker, is driven by a deep desire for inner and outer peace, striving to maintain harmony in their environment. They're valued for their ability to see various perspectives and create a peaceful atmosphere. Their main fear is being neglected, which often leads them to avoid confrontation. Their strength is their empathy and ability to create safe, open communication spaces, diffusing tension and uniting people. However, they must understand that conflict can't always be avoided and suppressing their needs isn't beneficial. Their voice and needs are important and asserting themselves is essential. They contribute to unity and peace, positively impacting others with their harmonious approach. Embracing their role as a Peacemaker allows them to foster understanding, empathy, and tranquility.

FREQUENTLY ASKED QUESTIONS

How Do the Core Motivations and Fears of Each Enneagram Type Impact Their Relationships With Others?

Ever thought about how your deepest desires and fears influence your relationships? It's all about understanding how these elements shape your actions. When you truly get your needs and fears, you can connect better with what drives others. Knowing this can help build stronger ties, filled with understanding and kindness. It's all about mastering the art of relationships with more understanding and tact.

Are There Any Specific Career Paths or Industries That Are More Suited to Each Enneagram Type Based on Their Core Motivations?

Ever thought if some careers or industries match your personal motivations better? Well, they do. Your unique enneagram type can naturally tilt you towards certain fields. But let's not forget, your personal interests and skills also matter. When you align your core motivations with a suitable job, it can lead you to satisfaction and success. So, dive in, discover your motivations, and start paving your way to a fulfilling career.

Can Someone's Enneagram Type Change Over Time, or Is It Fixed Throughout Their Life?

Is it possible for your Enneagram type to change or does it stay the same forever? Think about this: your personality is like a river, always changing and evolving. In the same way, your Enneagram type can also change. Life experiences and self-reflection can help you uncover different parts of yourself. So, don't be afraid of change, it's always possible. Embrace the journey of self-discovery.

Are There Any Common Patterns or Behaviors That Can Help Identify Someone's Enneagram Type Without Taking a Formal Assessment?

Want to figure out your Enneagram type without an official test? Just look closely at your everyday behaviors. Ask yourself what drives you and what scares you. Think about how you handle stress and the tactics you use to cope. Look at your relationships and see if you spot any common themes. Self-awareness is the magic word here. Spend time thinking about your thoughts, feelings, and actions. This will give you a good idea about your Enneagram type. Remember, understanding yourself is a journey, but with attention and patience, you'll get there.

How Do the Core Motivations and Fears of Each Enneagram Type Manifest in Their Daily Lives and Decision-Making Processes?

Let's talk about how your core motivations and fears show up in your everyday life and the choices you make. You see, these deep-seated forces guide your actions and decisions. By understanding what drives you, you can get a handle on why you act the way you do. And knowing your fears? That's the first step to beating them and living a life that's even more rewarding. So, let's dive in and start making more aware choices today.

CHAPTER 5
ENNEAGRAM CENTERS OF INTELLIGENCE

Inside of you there are three centers of intelligence - the head, the heart, and the gut, and they hold the keys to understanding yourself better. In this chapter, we'll dive into what each center does and how they shape our Enneagram types. By getting to know the power of the head, heart, and gut, you'll unlock precious insights into your own self. This will not only empower you but will also allow you to connect with others on a deeper level.

HEAD CENTER: UNDERSTANDING THE INTELLECT

Exploring the Head Center in the Enneagram helps understand your intellectual potential and how it can be used for the benefit of others. The Head Center, one of the three Centers of Intelligence, focuses on thinking, analyzing, and information processing. Those aligned with this center have an innate desire for clarity and understanding, excelling in logical reasoning, problem-solving, strategic thinking, and knowledge seeking.

However, an imbalance in intellectual capacities can lead to overthinking, anxiety, and mental loops, hindering effective service to others due to paralysis from over-analysis. Cultivating self-awareness and mindfulness, understanding intellectual strengths and weaknesses, and balancing thinking with action, are crucial for leveraging the Head Center's power.

HEART CENTER: EXPLORING EMOTIONS AND RELATIONSHIPS

The Heart Center of the Enneagram is an exploration of emotions and relationships, building on intellectual potential. It's where emotional connection, empathy, and deep relationship-building occur. Aspects of the Heart Center include:

- **Emotional Awareness**: Crucial for developing emotional intelligence, awareness of your own emotions and their influence on your thoughts and behaviors enables better relationship navigation. Expressing emotions fosters empathy and understanding.
- **Authenticity and Vulnerability**: Key for forming genuine relationships, authenticity is about being truthful to oneself and expressing emotions and needs honestly. Embracing vulnerability allows

others to see your true self, fostering trust and intimacy.

- **Compassionate Service**: The Heart Center drives the desire to serve others, finding fulfillment in supporting those around you. It involves active listening, offering support, and being there in times of need. This fosters strong connections and community well-being.

Exploring the Heart Center deepens emotional intelligence, builds authentic relationships, and promotes compassionate service, enhancing your ability to connect with others and positively impact their lives.

GUT CENTER: UNCOVERING INSTINCTS AND INTUITION

Discover the potency of your instincts and intuition in the Enneagram's Gut Center, also known as the body center, which is the birthplace of your physical sensations and instinctual reactions. Through understanding and engaging this center, you can enhance self-awareness and make choices that benefit others.

The Gut Center pertains to types 8, 9, and 1 of the Enneagram. If these types resonate with you, you likely lean on your intuition for guidance. While your intuition is a powerful navigation tool, it's crucial to differentiate between healthy instincts and reactive impulses. Increasing self-awareness and trusting your intuition can aid in this distinction.

To harness your instinctual power, connect with your body and observe your physical sensations. If your gut feels tight or uneasy, it might signify a misalignment with your values. Conversely, gut feelings of expansion or openness may imply you're on the right track.

HOW THE HEAD CENTER INFLUENCES ENNEAGRAM TYPES

The Head Center significantly impacts Enneagram types 5, 6, and 7 by molding their thought processes and decisions. Its influence manifests in three main ways:

- Overthinking: Those in this center often overanalyze situations, leading to decision paralysis. Learning to trust your intuition when you find yourself continually doubting your decisions can counteract this.
- Fear and anxiety: The Head Center is prone to worry and anxiety. It's vital to confront these fears directly and implement effective coping strategies.
- Pursuit of knowledge: The Head Center types are motivated by a desire for understanding and frequently seek information for security and control. Using this curiosity for personal growth is beneficial, but be wary of an endless knowledge-seeking cycle without action.

Recognizing the Head Center's influence can help you identify your thought patterns and make more mindful decisions. Addressing overthinking, fear, and incessant knowledge-seeking can lead to a healthier mindset and more satisfying life. Remember, self-care is the first step in serving others.

THE ROLE OF THE HEART AND GUT CENTERS IN ENNEAGRAM TYPES

The Heart and Gut Centers significantly influence Enneagram types. The Heart or Feeling Center governs emotions, desires, and interpersonal bonds. Dominant Heart Center individuals are likely Types Two, Three, or Four.

Type Twos, or Helpers, desire to serve others, showing empathy and attentiveness. Type Threes, the Achievers, seek success and recognition, excelling in emotional connectivity and relationship building. Type Fours, the Individualists, are deeply in tune with their own and others' emotions, longing for understanding and expressing their unique identities.

The Gut or Instinctive Center manages our instincts and physical reactions, creating intuition and gut feelings. Dominant Gut Center individuals are typically Types Eight, Nine, or One.

Type Eights, the Challengers, are driven by control and power, marked by assertiveness and decisiveness. Type Nines, the Peacemakers, desire inner and outer peace, using their strong gut feelings to navigate conflicts and create harmony. Type Ones, the Perfectionists, have a need for order and moral integrity, using their gut instinct to make principled decisions and strive for perfection.

FREQUENTLY ASKED QUESTIONS

How Does the Head Center Relate to Decision-Making and Problem-Solving?

When you're making decisions or trying to solve problems, your head center is your best friend. It's the part of you that's all about logic and intellect. It's what helps you sort through details, weigh your options, and make smart decisions. It lets you think clearly and find down-to-earth solutions to whatever you're facing. By really tuning into this part of yourself, you can trust your gut and make decisions that truly help others. Pretty cool, right?

Are There Any Specific Enneagram Types That Are More Commonly Associated With the Heart Center?

Did you know that specific Enneagram types are tied more closely to the heart center? Let's take a quick look at Type 2, also known as the Helper. They're known for their strong desire to help others and their effortless connection with their emotions. It's love and appreciation that fuels their actions. What really stands out is their knack for empathy and meeting others' needs. They truly excel in this. Pretty cool, huh?

Can the Gut Center Be Considered the Primary Center of Intelligence in Some Individuals?

Absolutely! In some people, the gut can indeed be the main source of smarts. Your gut feelings are strong and can help you make swift, firm choices. When you trust your gut, you're tapping into your intuition and deep-seated knowledge. So, if you notice that your gut reactions are often spot on, then your gut could well be your key intelligence hub.

What Role Do Emotions Play in the Head Center's Functioning?

Emotions are really important when it comes to how our minds work. They're like our personal navigational system, helping us make choices and decisions. You know how a lighthouse helps ships find their way in a storm? That's what our emotions do for us - they light up the way forward, especially when things are uncertain. When we listen to our feelings and let them guide us, we're able to tap into a wisdom that's deeper than just our intellect. So don't shy away from your emotions. Embrace them. They're your key to unlocking your true smarts.

Are There Any Enneagram Types That Rely Equally on All Three Centers of Intelligence?

Do any enneagram types balance all three centers of intelligence? Absolutely! Some folks have managed to harmonize their head, heart, and gut centers. They can think sharply, feel intensely, and rely on their gut feelings. This balance helps them to make choices that reflect their values, intuition, and logical thinking. They show us how we can also create balance in our own centers of intelligence.

CONCLUSION

The Enneagram centers of intelligence, namely the head, heart, and gut, are like a beautiful symphony, where each center has its own unique part to play in moulding who we are. And, just like a skilled conductor, we need to create a balance between these centers to truly unleash our potential. By diving into our minds, exploring our feelings and relationships, and tapping into our instincts and intuition, we step into a journey of self-discovery and personal growth.

CHAPTER 6
ENNEAGRAM WINGS

Ever felt like there's more to your Enneagram type than meets the eye? Ready to discover what's lurking below the surface? Let's plunge into the next chapter of your Enneagram journey - the world of wings. These wings, nestled beside your main Enneagram type, offer a richer insight into how your primary type links with others. Think of them as the special seasoning that adds depth to your personality, making it even more vibrant and sophisticated. Let's see how these wings can rewrite your unique tale.

ENNEAGRAM TYPE 1 WINGS

Let's explore the wings of Enneagram Type 1, also known as The Reformer. The two wing options for Type 1 are 1w2 and 1w9. Each wing brings its own unique flavor and influences the traits of the Type 1, adding depth and complexity to their personality. Under-standing these wings can provide a more comprehensive understanding of Type 1 individuals and their motivations, fears, and desires.

About Enneagram 1w2

Enneagram 1w2 (Enneagram Type 1 Wings) helps reveal nuanced traits of the Reformer type. As a 1w2 individual, you have a strong drive to serve others and maintain moral righteousness, enhanced by the nurturing qualities of the Helper wing. You aim for perfection and high standards, but also possess a caring nature that prompts you to help others. Your focus on justice and fairness is tempered by your empathetic and supportive nature. Understanding your 1w2 wing allows you to comprehend these traits within your personality and utilize them to positively affect others.

About Enneagram 1w9

Enneagram 1w9 combines the Reformer's desire for structure and perfection with a quest for peace and harmony. As a 1w9, you pursue order and perfection, yet also prioritize inner tranquility and harmonious environments. Driven by a need for justice, you aim to bring balance and calm to your relationships and surroundings. Diplomatic and empathetic, you peacefully resolve conflicts. Your Type 1 tendencies encourage high standards and discipline, but your 9 wing introduces adaptability, facilitating compromise and calm in your perfection pursuit.

ENNEAGRAM TYPE 2 WINGS

Now let's talk about the Enneagram Type 2 wings, specifically the 2w1 and 2w3. These wings add different flavors to the Helper type, enhancing or diminishing certain traits. Understanding these wings will give you a more accurate and precise profile, allowing you to delve deeper into your personality story.

About Enneagram 2w1

Enneagram 2w1 is a personality type that amalgamates the traits of Type 2 and Type 1. This type is characterized by a strong drive to aid others, coupled with high regard for integrity and morality. Key attributes include a natural propensity to support others, balanced by a robust sense of ethics and the importance of personal integrity. They work towards fostering harmonious relationships and bring order in their associations. Guided by a stern moral compass, they find satisfaction in championing justice and fairness. Their motivation stems from deep empathy and the desire for a positive global impact. Thus, an Enneagram 2w1, with their blend of empathy, helpfulness, and integrity, is a significant contributor to their community.

About Enneagram 2w3

Enneagram 2w3, also termed as Enneagram Type 2 Wings, blends the characteristics of Type 2 and 3. As a 2w3, you're driven by a desire to help others and influence the world positively, often prioritizing others' needs over yours due to your compassionate, empathetic, and nurturing nature. Your Type 3 influence injects ambition into your personality, facilitating your knack for charming and impressing others, which aids in relationship building and goal achievement. You seek acknowledgement for your service-oriented efforts. Your mix of selflessness and ambition positions you to significantly impact others' lives.

ENNEAGRAM TYPE 3 WINGS

Let's look at the two wing options for Enneagram Type 3: 3w2 and 3w4. The 3w2 wing brings a focus on relationships and a desire to be liked and admired, while the 3w4 wing adds a touch of individuality and a drive for uniqueness. Understanding these wing options can help you gain insight into the different aspects of Type 3 and how they manifest in your personality.

About Enneagram 3w2

Enneagram 3w2 combines Type 3's drive and ambition with Type 2's charm and relatability. As a 3w2, you're ambitious, adaptable, charming, and adept at relationship-building. You prioritize others' needs, seek validation, and strive for competency. Balancing your needs with others' can be challenging. Your ambition and drive can significantly impact others by serving and uplifting them.

About Enneagram 3w4

Enneagram 3w4 combines Type 3's ambition with Type 4's individualism and depth. As a 3w4, you crave success and recognition, driven by a desire for uniqueness and authenticity in your endeavors. Your 4 wing introduces introspection and emotional depth, enabling self-exploration and deep connections with others. You possess a innate ability to inspire and positively impact others through your ambition and individuality.

ENNEAGRAM TYPE 4 WINGS

Let's explore the wings of Enneagram Type 4, the Individualist. In particular, we will discuss the characteristics and dynamics of both 4w3 and 4w5. Understanding these wing options will provide insight into how they enhance or influence the core traits of Type 4, and how they shape the overall personality of individuals with Type 4 as their dominant type.

About Enneagram 4w3

Explore the distinct traits of the 4w3 Enneagram type and how its wings influence its personality. The 4w3 type merges Type 4's individualism with Type 3's ambition and image-consciousness, resulting in a personality that aspires for uniqueness, success, and recognition.

Key features of 4w3 include creativity, emotional sensitivity, authenticity, ambition, and a desire for admiration. The 3 wing fuels competitiveness, a longing for external validation, and a focus on maintaining a positive image.

Understanding the 4w3 Enneagram can guide individuals within this classification to balance their pursuit of authenticity and success while preserving their unique identity.

About Enneagram 4w5

Exploring Enneagram 4w3 further, we now focus on Enneagram 4w5, another wing for Type 4 personalities. Type 4 with a 4w5 wing merges unique traits, adding intellectual and introspective depth to an already sensitive nature. You express individuality through creative outlets like art and writing, complemented by an analytical mindset from your 5 wing, leading to curiosity and a thirst for knowledge. There might be a tendency to retreat to contemplate emotions and thoughts. Your blend of creativity and intellect can serve others well, offering understanding and empathy.

ENNEAGRAM TYPE 5 WINGS

Let's explore the wings of Enneagram Type 5. As a Type 5, you have two wing options: 5w4 and 5w6. Understanding these wings will provide insights into how they influence your dominant type and add unique flavor to your personality. By examining the characteristics of both wings, you can gain a deeper understanding of yourself and navigate personal growth and development more effectively.

About Enneagram 5w4

Enneagram 5w4, or Type 5 with a 4 wing, is a personality type that combines Type 5's introspective, observant nature with Type 4's individualistic, creative traits. Key characteristics of 5w4 include a rich inner life, a thirst for knowledge, and a creative, analytical mindset. They often take an artistic or unconventional approach to problem-solving. While they value independence and alone time for reflection, they might find it hard to balance their need for privacy with a desire for connection and belonging. Understanding this unique personality type can help in supporting their pursuit of knowledge and self-expression.

About Enneagram 5w6

Enneagram 5w6, or the 'Troubleshooter', has key differences from Enneagram 5w4. Like 5w4, 5w6 focuses on knowledge acquisition and understanding the world, but it also incorporates a secondary wing of 6, which brings loyalty, responsibility, and a service-oriented nature. Unlike 5w4, 5w6 is not just about personal knowledge gain, but also assisting others. Its analytical, detail-oriented, and problem-solving skills make it a valuable resource. It aims to provide stability and security while preserving its privacy and independence. This blend of intellectual curiosity and empathy can greatly benefit those it serves.

ENNEAGRAM TYPE 6 WINGS

Now it's time to explore the wings of Enneagram Type 6. Your wings can greatly influence your personality and behavior, adding unique nuances to your dominant type. Understanding the characteristics of both Enneagram 6w5 and 6w7 will give you a more comprehensive understanding of yourself and how you navigate the world. Let's delve into the distinct traits and qualities of each wing to uncover a deeper understanding of your Enneagram Type 6.

About Enneagram 6w5

Exploring your Enneagram wing, like the 6w5 for Type 6 or the Loyalist, can enrich your self-understanding. Key strengths of the 6w5 include sharp analytical abilities, profound introspection, and independence. Challenges encompass overthinking, trust issues, and decision-making fears. Comprehending your 6w5 wing aids in balanced navigation of life, equipping you to analyze scenarios, trust your gut, and confront your fears. Embracing strengths and addressing challenges allows you to serve others with your unique blend of loyalty and insight. Knowledge of your wing and main type provides a comprehensive view of your enneatype.

About Enneagram 6w7

The Enneagram 6w7 combines traits from Type 6 and 7. As a 6w7, you're loyal, responsible, and cautious, but also adventurous, spontaneous, and enthusiastic due to your 7 wing. This wing helps balance your Type 6 anxieties with optimism and excitement. Your personality shines in your service to others, offering support, guidance, and a sense of joy. Navigating challenges with practicality and adventure, you're a valuable asset in serving others.

ENNEAGRAM TYPE 7 WINGS

Now let's talk about Enneagram Type 7 Wings. As a Type 7, you have two wing options: 7w6 and 7w8. Your wing enhances or diminishes certain traits of your main type, adding a unique flavor to your personality. Understanding your wing can provide a deeper understanding of your motivations and behaviors as a Type 7.

About Enneagram 7w6

Examining Enneagram 7w6, or Enneagram Type 7 Wings, reveals a dynamic, adventurous personality. Key traits include:

- Enthusiasm and sociability: 7w6s have a zest for life and enjoy socializing. Their outgoing nature makes them enjoyable companions.
- Desire for new experiences: 7w6s have a strong appetite for novelty and variety, constantly seeking new places, activities, and opportunities.

These traits enable 7w6s to energize and inspire others with their adventurous spirit, making them a valuable asset in social or service-oriented environments.

About Enneagram 7w8

Enneagram 7w8 reflects a lively personality characterized by the adventurous optimism of Type 7, enhanced by the assertiveness of Type 8. As a 7w8, you are motivated by freedom, novelty, and thrill, exhibiting an energetic, sociable demeanor that attracts others. You excel at finding joy in the present, but you must be wary of your tendency to dodge pain and discomfort, which can incite impulsivity and commitment-phobia. Utilizing your Type 8 wing can foster a robust sense of self and assertiveness, equipping you to tackle challenges bravely. However, it's vital to couple your adventurousness with a grounded sense of responsibility and empathy.

ENNEAGRAM TYPE 8 WINGS

Let's explore the wings of Enneagram Type 8. The two wing options for Type 8 are 8w7 and 8w9. The wing you rely on the most influences and enhances your dominant Type 8 traits, bringing a unique flavor to your personality.

About Enneagram 8w7

Enneagram Type 8w7 blends the forcefulness of Type 8 with the excitement of Type 7. As an 8w7, you have the following key traits:

- You're a natural leader, motivated by power and a love for exploration.
- Your protective instinct is coupled with a joyous, spontaneous approach to life.
- You value justice and fairness and aren't afraid to challenge authority.
- Your decision-making skills are paired with a longing for freedom and diversity.

- You exhibit confidence and self-assurance, balanced with humor and light-heartedness.

As an 8w7, your strength, determination, and love for life make you a unique leader, eager to take risks and seek adventure. Use your assertiveness and power to positively influence others.

About Enneagram 8w9

As an Enneagram 8w9, you blend the power and protectiveness of Type 8 with the peacefulness of Type 9. You're focused on safeguarding others, using your strength and assertiveness for making a safe environment. Unlike the more aggressive 8w7, you maintain calm and seek harmony. You value peace, aim to foster strong connections and unity among those around you. Your balanced strength and relaxed attitude make you a dependable ally. Understanding your 8w9 wings can enhance your ability to empathetically serve others.

ENNEAGRAM TYPE 9 WINGS

Now let's explore the Enneagram Type 9 Wings, specifically the 9w8 and 9w1. Understanding these wings will give you a deeper understanding of the Enneagram Type 9 and how they interact with their dominant type. The 9w8 brings a touch of assertiveness and strength to the easy-going nature of Type 9, while the 9w1 adds a sense of idealism and perfectionism.

About Enneagram 9w8

Enneagram 9w8, a combination of the peaceful Type 9 and assertive Type 8, uniquely blends calmness and self-confidence. These individuals seek harmony, but won't hesitate to fight for their or others' rights. They excel at mediating conflicts and asserting their own needs, valuing service to others and fostering a balanced environment. Their calming presence and diplomatic skill are effective in easing tense situations. Understanding the 9w8 Enneagram offers valuable insight into these distinct qualities.

About Enneagram 9w1

Understanding your Enneagram Type 9w1 involves recognizing your traits and tendencies. You are typically calm and aim to sustain peace, driven by a strong moral compass. You value service to others and derive joy from providing aid and support. However, you may face tension between your peace-seeking nature and need for self-assertion. Balancing these needs is crucial for your growth. Acknowledging your wing can lead to deeper self-awareness and empathy in relationships.

UNDERSTANDING ENNEAGRAM WINGS

Now it's time to understand how Enneagram wings influence each type. Your Enneagram type is not just defined by your core type, but also by the influence of your wing. The combination of your core type and wing creates a unique personality pattern, and exploring these wing combinations can provide deeper insight into your motivations, behaviors, and growth opportunities.

Wing Influence on Types

Explore the impact of Enneagram wings on your personality type. Wings, the neighboring types on the Enneagram diagram, add depth to your primary type, influencing your behavior and motivations in four main ways:

1. **Balancing**: Wings can counterbalance your primary type's extreme tendencies.
2. **Enhancing**: Wings can amplify specific traits of your primary type.
3. **Growth**: Wings can foster personal growth by developing less dominant qualities of your primary type.
4. **Challenges**: Wings can unearth conflicting desires or motivations, prompting self-exploration and conflict resolution.

Gaining understanding of your wing's influence can provide insights into your development and personal growth, ultimately improving your ability to serve others.

Exploring Wing Combinations

Exploring Enneagram wing combinations is crucial in understanding your personality. Each Enneagram type has two wings that shape your primary type and provide insights into behavior, motivations, and growth potential. Identifying your wing combination can highlight unique strengths and improvement areas. For instance, a

Type Two with a Three wing may have natural charisma and a drive to assist others, while a Two with a One wing might show perfectionism and fairness. Understanding your wing combination can enhance your self-awareness and personal growth, guiding you to become the best version of yourself.

HOW WINGS INFLUENCE ENNEAGRAM TYPES

Understand the significant role wings play in shaping Enneagram types to enhance your personal growth and service to others. Wings impact Enneagram types in four crucial ways:

1. **Strengthening your qualities:** Wings bolster your primary Enneagram type by introducing complementary traits, providing extra skills and viewpoints beneficial in personal and professional relationships.
2. **Counterbalancing your faults:** Wings help to counterbalance the difficult aspects of your main type, enabling you to handle tough situations with greater grace and resilience.
3. **Adding complexity:** Wings introduce depth to your Enneagram type, leading to a more intricate understanding of your personality. They add layers to your core motivations, aiding you in uncovering your subtle behavioral and thought nuances.

4. **Promoting growth and integration:** Exploration of your wings can foster personal growth and integration, expanding your behavior range and unlocking potential. This contributes to a more balanced self, improving your effectiveness and wisdom in serving others.

INTEGRATING AND BALANCING ENNEAGRAM WINGS

To enhance personal growth and manage challenges effectively, it's crucial to integrate and balance your Enneagram wings. This process involves using the strengths of your dominant type and its wings to foster a balanced personality. Begin by identifying the motivations and fears of each wing and understand how they align or conflict with your dominant type.

To balance your wings, be aware of any tendency to rely too heavily on one over the other, which can lead to rigidity or scattered thoughts. Address this imbalance by consciously seeking equilibrium between your wings.

Mindfulness and self-reflection are practical ways to integrate and balance your wings. Daily observation of your thoughts, emotions, and behaviors, and noticing any excessive leaning towards one wing can help you bring in the qualities of the other wing, promoting flexibility and adaptability.

DEVELOPING AWARENESS OF ENNEAGRAM WINGS

To develop awareness of your Enneagram wings, it is important to understand the dynamics of these wings and how they influence your personality. By exploring the influences of your wings, you can gain valuable insights into your behavior and motivations. Embrace your personal wing as an integral part of your Enneagram type, and use this knowledge to further your personal growth and self-awareness.

Understanding Wing Dynamics

In studying Enneagram wings, it's crucial to grasp how they shape each personality type. The four critical aspects of wing dynamics are:

1. Wings add extra traits: Your main wing incorporates features from adjacent types, enhancing your self-understanding and shedding light on your actions and motivations.
2. Wings establish equilibrium: Your wing can temper the extreme tendencies of your primary type, encouraging a balanced life approach.
3. Wings heighten certain qualities: Your wing can emphasize strengths or weaknesses related to your primary type, leading to a more definite Enneagram expression.
4. Wings promote individual growth: Recognizing your wing dynamics enables you to utilize the strengths of your primary type and wing,

allowing for personality development and improvement.

Exploring Wing Influences

Exploring the impact of Enneagram wings on each personality type enhances your understanding of their role in shaping your unique expression. This is a crucial step in your journey of self-discovery and personal growth. The wings, represented by the two adjacent numbers on the Enneagram symbol, add complexity to your core type by offering additional traits that influence your interactions. By understanding your wing influences, you gain insights into your strengths, weaknesses, and motivations, enabling you to interact more effectively and make better decisions. This awareness helps you achieve balance and guides you towards a fulfilling life.

Embracing Personal Wing

Begin by understanding and accepting your personal wing to deepen your awareness of its impact on your Enneagram type. Recognizing your wing offers insights into your character and behaviors, aiding your self-discovery and growth. Here are four reasons why this is crucial:

1. Self-Awareness: Accepting your wing helps you better comprehend your strengths, weaknesses, and motivations, enabling you to make choices that reflect your true self.

2. Compassion: Accepting your wing fosters empathy for others with your Enneagram type, improving your ability to connect and serve.

3. Growth Opportunities: Your wing provides qualities that can enrich or challenge your dominant type, presenting opportunities for development.

4. Integration: Accepting your wing is vital for fully embodying your Enneagram type, bringing balance to your character for a more authentic life.

The process of accepting your personal wing involves self-reflection, curiosity, and openness, helping you tap into your Enneagram type's full potential and live a purposeful life.

FREQUENTLY ASKED QUESTIONS

How Do Enneagram Wings Affect Relationships With Others?

Enneagram wings can really shape your connections with folks. Think of them as two extra personality traits that guide how you relate to others. They can make or break your relationships - it's all in how you use them. Get to know your wings and you'll have a clearer view of yourself and how you deal with relationships. If you can recognize and juggle the strong and weak points of your wings, you'll be able to build stronger, more rewarding relationships. Go for it!

Can Someone Have More Than One Wing?

Absolutely, you can have more than one wing in the Enneagram system. Your main type is still your personality's core, but with two wings, you can tap into the strengths and traits of both. It's like having an extra tool kit, helping you handle various situations. Think of it as being a bird with two wings, letting you fly higher and explore your personality in new ways. You've got this!

Do Enneagram Wings Change Over Time?

Let's talk about Enneagram wings. These are the two types right next to your main one, and they don't change as time goes by. They stick with you for life, adding unique traits and behaviors that match your core type. Think of these wings as your personal support crew, giving you fresh viewpoints and ways to tackle life's ups and downs. Even though your main type stays the same, your wings mold and boost your personality. They help you to learn, grow, and flourish within your Enneagram type. Pretty cool, right?

What Are Some Common Misconceptions About Enneagram Wings?

You might have heard some misconceptions about Enneagram wings, like they're set in stone or solely shape your personality. But here's the real deal - your wings can change and grow over time, and they're just one part of your overall Enneagram type. Sure, they add some extra color to your personality, but they don't define you entirely. Think of your Enneagram journey as an exciting path of growth and change. It's all about evolving, not being stuck in one box.

How Can Understanding Enneagram Wings Help in Personal Growth and Self-Awareness?

Knowing your enneagram wings can really boost your personal growth and self-awareness. When you understand your wing, you get a clear view of your personality's unique quirks and tendencies. This helps you see your strengths and weaknesses. And guess what? It's a powerful tool. You can use this knowledge to make decisions that truly reflect who you are. This leads to personal growth and a better understanding of your motivations and behaviors. So, let's dive in and embrace this opportunity for self-discovery and personal growth.

CONCLUSION

When you're exploring your Enneagram type, don't forget to check out your wings. Think of them as the extra splash of color that makes your personality pop. They show off the best parts of you and tell your unique story. So, don't be shy, let your wings fly. They're a big part of what makes you, you.

CHAPTER 7
THE ENNEAGRAM SUBTYPES

Ready to peel back the layers of your personality? This chapter on Enneagram subtypes will take you on an enlightening journey. You'll explore how these subtypes highlight your deepest yearnings and drivers. The nine types each have three unique subtypes that shape how you interact with the world. So, let's set off on this exciting exploration of self-discovery and see which subtype aligns with your caring personality.

TYPE 1: SELF PRESERVATION, SOCIAL, SEXUAL

In the Enneagram system's Type 1, three different subtypes exist: Self Preservation, Social, and Sexual. Each provides a unique means of serving others.

The Self Preservation subtype prioritizes personal wellness to serve others effectively, focusing on maintaining well-being and meeting basic needs. This approach ensures personal energy and stability, contributing to a comfortable and secure environment for all.

The Social subtype centers on community connection and service. It harnesses the power of bringing people together, fostering belonging, and positively impacting society. This subtype's sense of responsibility and service commitment motivates others to join them.

The Sexual subtype is marked by a potent passion in service, striving for significant global impact. It encourages personal growth and transformation, preferring deep, meaningful relationships over superficial connections.

TYPE 2: SELF PRESERVATION, SOCIAL, SEXUAL

When it comes to Type 2, the self-preservation subtype focuses on meeting their own needs first, ensuring their well-being before helping others. The social subtype, on the other hand, thrives on forming connections and relationships within their community, always being there for others. Lastly, the sexual subtype brings intensity and passion into their relationships, seeking deep emotional connections and often being more assertive in expressing their desires. Each subtype influences the motivations and behaviors of Type 2 individuals in different ways.

Different Subtype Influences

Understanding the influence of self-preservation, social, and sexual subtypes on Type 2 individuals is crucial.

- Self-Preservation subtype in Type 2 focuses on self-care before serving others, prioritizing personal physical and emotional health, and seeking comfort and security in relationships.
- Social subtype Type 2 individuals aim for community acceptance and value, tuning into others' needs and expectations, striving for indispensability, and excelling at network creation and fostering belonging.
- Sexual subtype Type 2 individuals are intense and passionate in relationships, seek deep emotional connections, and may exhibit possessiveness or jealousy. Their need for intimacy and desire to be desired can be consuming.

Recognizing these influences can aid Type 2 individuals in aligning their relationships and service to others with their unique traits.

Impact on Motivations

As a Type 2, understanding the effects of self-preservation, social, and sexual subtypes on your motivations is crucial. These subtypes shape your actions and intentions. Self-preservation subtype focuses on self-care to serve others effectively. The social subtype underlines the significance of connection and community, motivating you to build relationships. The sexual subtype adds intensity to your interactions, enhancing your desire to be needed and loved. Awareness of these subtypes helps understand your motivations and their impact on your service to others.

TYPE 3: SELF PRESERVATION, SOCIAL, SEXUAL

Understanding the Enneagram Type 3 involves exploring its three subtypes: Self Preservation, Social, and Sexual, which reveal how these individuals interact with the world.

- **Self Preservation**: This subtype focuses on personal well-being and security, striving for success to ensure a comfortable life for themselves and their loved ones. These individuals are ambitious, driven, and resourceful.
- **Social**: Those with this subtype prioritize relationships and social standing, excelling at networking, connection-building, and image creation. They adapt well to social scenarios and are often seen as charismatic leaders.
- **Sexual**: Characterized by a strong drive for personal achievement, this subtype is competitive, ambitious, and risk-taking. They have a natural charisma that attracts others, making them effective leaders.

These subtypes help identify how Type 3 individuals aim to serve others, whether through a focus on personal well-being, relationship building, or personal success.

Understanding these approaches allows for better collaboration and support of Type 3 individuals in their service to others.

TYPE 4: SELF PRESERVATION, SOCIAL, SEXUAL

Type 4 individuals' self-preservation subtype drives their need to prioritize personal well-being, essential for serving others effectively. This often results in creating a comfortable, aesthetically pleasing environment fostering emotional expressivity and creativity. The social subtype exhibits a profound desire for connection and belonging, thriving in communities where unique perspectives are shared. Their authenticity, sensitivity, and empathetic nature foster deep relationships and garner support and validation. The sexual subtype radiates a powerful urge for intimacy and intensity in relationships, seeking partners who can match their emotional depth and passion. This often leads to a constant pursuit of deep, soulful connections and a willingness to risk and explore new experiences. In essence, a Type 4 individual's subtypes focus on self-preservation, social connectivity, and intense emotional experiences, enabling more authentic engagement with the world and better navigation of relationships.

TYPE 5: SELF PRESERVATION, SOCIAL, SEXUAL

The self-preservation subtype of Type 5 individuals influences their approach to personal health and effective service to others in three main ways. Firstly, they prioritize their physical and emotional well-being, setting boundaries and dedicating time to self-care activities. Secondly, although typically introverted, they strive to balance solitude with meaningful social interactions, enabling them to effectively engage with others. Lastly, their strong drive for knowledge and mastery helps them provide valuable insights and solutions, serving others effectively. Thus, by focusing on self-care, balancing solitude and connection, and deepening their expertise, Type 5 individuals with the self-preservation subtype can serve others from a position of strength and wisdom.

TYPE 6: SELF PRESERVATION, SOCIAL, SEXUAL

As a self-preservation Type 6, you use your instincts and deep relationships to handle life's complexities. Ensuring your own safety and being prepared for potential threats is your primary focus. Your heightened sense of self-preservation sees you prioritizing your physical needs and being practical and cautious in your approach to life.

Your relationships hold great importance for you, as you seek belonging and community, thriving on trust and security within your social group. Your sexual instinct influences your behavior and motivations, marked by a desire for intense, passionate relationships and experiences that create emotional intimacy.

In essence, as a self-preservation, social, sexual Type 6, you rely on your instincts and relationships to navigate life, prioritizing your safety while seeking belonging and intense connections. Understanding these aspects of your personality enables you to grow and serve others in sync with your desires and values.

TYPE 7: SELF PRESERVATION, SOCIAL, SEXUAL

Now it's time to explore the variations in Type 7 through its subtypes: Self Preservation, Social, and Sexual. These subtypes have a significant impact on the way Type 7 individuals express themselves and navigate the world. Understanding the nuances of each subtype can provide valuable insights into the motivations, behaviors, and fears of Type 7s.

Subtype Variations in Type 7

The self-preservation, social, and sexual variations of Type 7 Enneagram characteristics each have unique features.

- Self-Preservation: Type 7s with this subtype focus on fulfilling personal needs and ensuring their comfort and security. They're often organized and resourceful, constantly seeking new experiences to satisfy their desires.

- Social: Social Type 7s value making connections and gaining others' approval. They flourish in social scenarios and enjoy being the center of attention. They continuously seek new relationships and experiences but may fear missing out and have commitment issues.
- Sexual: Sexual Type 7s crave intensity and passion in relationships. They're adventurous, always seeking new experiences and relationships. However, they may fear feeling trapped or limited in their relationships.

Understanding these Type 7 variations can aid in providing personalized support to individuals with different subtypes.

Impact of Subtype on Type 7

Understanding the effect of subtypes on Type 7 (Self Preservation, Social, Sexual) reveals unique traits and needs of these individuals. Self Preservation subtypes focus on personal comfort and security, potentially leading to impulsivity and materialism. Social subtypes prioritize social connections and activities, often fearing solitude and constantly seeking new experiences. Sexual subtypes are driven by strong desires, prone to risk-taking and pleasure-seeking. Recognizing these subtypes enhances our ability to cater to Type 7 personalities.

TYPE 8: SELF PRESERVATION, SOCIAL, SEXUAL

The self-preservation, social, and sexual instincts significantly shape your Type 8 personality, influencing your behavior, motivations, and relationships.

- The self-preservation instinct fuels your drive for safety, security, and well-being, making you prioritize your physical needs and fiercely control your environment. It may lead you to gather resources and guard what's yours.
- The social instinct makes you value relationships and collective well-being, leading you to take leadership roles and champion for justice and fairness. You're driven by the desire to serve your community and make a large-scale impact.
- The sexual instinct heightens your assertiveness and passion, resulting in a strong craving for deep connections and thrill in relationships. It gives you a compelling presence, and your ambition may be focused on fulfilling your desires and overcoming challenges.

Recognizing how these subtypes align with your Type 8 personality enhances self-awareness and helps in managing relationships. Balancing these instincts allows you to use their power to serve others and make a significant world impact.

TYPE 9: SELF PRESERVATION, SOCIAL, SEXUAL

Type 9 individuals' personalities are shaped by their self-preservation, social, and sexual instincts. The self-preservation instinct in Type 9s prioritizes personal well-being and peace, driving them towards stability and conflict avoidance. Socially inclined Type 9s seek connection and harmony in relationships, valuing community participation and striving to maintain peace. Those with sexual instincts crave deep, intimate connections, seeking intensity and passion in relationships, and may fear abandonment. Understanding these subtypes enhances comprehension of Type 9s' motivations and behaviors, facilitating supportive and fulfilling interactions.

FREQUENTLY ASKED QUESTIONS

How Do the Self-Preservation, Social, and Sexual Subtypes Differ Within Each Enneagram Type?

Let's dive into the world of enneagram types! You see, each type has three subtypes: self-preservation, social, and sexual. They each offer a unique lens on how we approach life, relationships, and even personal growth. For instance, if you're a self-preservation subtype, you're all about survival and practical needs. If you're more of a social subtype, you value connections and a sense of belonging. And for the sexual subtype, intensity and personal desires are key. Understanding these can really help you get to know yourself and others better. So, let's dig deeper into the enneagram and make life better for everyone around us, shall we?

Can a Person Exhibit Characteristics of More Than One Subtype Within Their Enneagram Type?

Curious about showing more than one subtype within your enneagram type? The answer is absolutely yes! Each one of us is unique, which means we can show traits from several subtypes. Think of the enneagram as a guide on your personal journey of discovery and growth. It celebrates our complexity as human beings. So, don't be afraid to explore the various subtypes within your enneagram type. Keep diving deep into your self-discovery, and enjoy every step of your personal growth!

Are Certain Subtypes More Common Among Certain Enneagram Types?

Sure, some Enneagram types often link to specific subtypes. The three subtypes, self-preservation, social, and sexual, shape how you show your type's main motives. Let's say you're a Type 1. If you're a self-preservation subtype, you might focus on your personal safety and health. If you're a social subtype, you might seek to connect with others and feel like you belong. If you're a sexual subtype, you could crave deep connections and intense experiences. By understanding your subtype, you can better grasp your unique way of expressing your Enneagram type. It's quite insightful!

How Do the Self-Preservation, Social, and Sexual Subtypes Affect Relationships and Interactions With Others?

When it comes to dealing with others, the Enneagram's self-preservation, social, and sexual subtypes can really shape things. If you're a self-preservation type, you might be more careful and realistic, always thinking about your own needs and safety. If you're more of a social subtype, you're likely to be the one who values relationships and cares about the community. Now, if you're a sexual subtype, you're all about intensity and passion in relationships, always seeking deep connections and intimate moments. These subtypes can help you understand yourself better and improve your interactions with others. So, keep exploring and growing!

Are There Any Common Patterns or Themes That Emerge Within Each Subtype Across All Enneagram Types?

Looking into the common trends in each Enneagram subtype can be really useful. It can help you understand the unique traits of each subtype and how they affect all types. This knowledge can better your relationships and interactions with others. It's like having a roadmap for understanding people's behaviors, including your own. Plus, it's a great way to build stronger, healthier connections with the people in your life. So, let's dig into these patterns and discover new ways to connect with others and ourselves.

CONCLUSION

Looking to get to know yourself better? Whether you identify as a Type 1 or a Type 9, the enneagram subtypes have a lot to reveal about you. They are like a trio of unique energies - self-preservation, social, and sexual, that shape and influence how we interact with the world. Think of it this way: the Self-Preservation subtype is like a meticulous planner, the Social subtype is like the life of the party, and the Sexual subtype brings passion and intensity. These subtypes add a dash of flavor to our personalities. So, why not take a deep dive into your type? You might be surprised by what you discover!

CHAPTER 8
THE ENNEAGRAM
LEVELS OF
DEVELOPMENT

Are you aware that knowing your Enneagram type can actually improve how you interact with others? Let's explore the captivating realm of the Enneagram Levels of Development: Healthy, Average, Unhealthy. In this chapter, we'll break down each level's traits and guide you to pinpoint your current position. Plus, we'll provide you with practical steps to progress towards growth and health. So, are you ready to delve into an adventure of self-discovery and purposeful living? It's time to master your Enneagram type and make a difference!

THE ENNEAGRAM LEVELS OF DEVELOPMENT EXPLAINED

The Enneagram's development levels offer a framework for understanding personality types and their behaviors. The healthy level is characterized by self-awareness, emotional balance, and a service-oriented mindset, utilizing virtues like compassion and wisdom. In the average level, individuals may become more self-focused and exhibit negative traits such as perfectionism or impatience, yet still have growth potential. The unhealthy level is marked by extreme negative behavior patterns and emotional strife, but growth remains possible with proper support. Understanding these levels can highlight your current position and guide personal growth, enabling you to better embody your type's positive traits and serve others effectively.

UNDERSTANDING THE HEALTHY LEVEL OF DEVELOPMENT

To comprehend the healthy development level in the Enneagram, cultivate self-awareness and a service-oriented approach. A healthy mindset enhances your capacity to serve others significantly. The four critical elements to achieve this include:

- **Self-reflection:** Engaging in deep introspection helps you understand your motivations and values. By understanding your thoughts and behaviors, you can serve others effectively.
- **Empathy:** Actively listening and understanding others' perspectives enhances empathy. This helps you connect deeply with others and provide meaningful support.
- **Compassion:** The key to serving others is compassion, which involves genuine concern for others and actions to ease their suffering. Practice

compassion by seeking opportunities to help the needy and exhibiting kindness.

- **Boundaries:** Establishing healthy boundaries is as important as serving others. Knowing your limits helps you serve others sustainably and equitably.

CHARACTERISTICS OF THE AVERAGE LEVEL OF DEVELOPMENT

Transitioning from the healthy level of Enneagram development to the average level involves a strong desire to positively impact others driven by duty and responsibility. This stage may increase self-consciousness and a need for validation, often prioritizing others' needs over your own, which may lead to struggles with setting personal boundaries.

You may also become more aware of your flaws, leading to self-criticism, guilt, and fear of judgement. Despite these issues, your empathy and compassion are evident as you are dedicated to understanding and meeting others' needs, even at your own expense.

SIGNS OF AN UNHEALTHY LEVEL OF DEVELOPMENT

Unhealthy development levels can negatively impact your well-being. Indicators include:

- **Lack of self-awareness:** You may feel detached from your actual emotions and aims, struggling to understand your needs while catering only to others.
- **Extreme behavior:** You may display behaviors not in line with your fundamental values, such as being overly aggressive, deceitful, or self-destructive.
- **Difficulty in relationships:** Unhealthy growth can affect your relationships, leading to struggles in maintaining healthy boundaries and causing over-dependence or aloofness. This can erode trust and communication.
- **Feeling overwhelmed:** You might feel burdened by stress and responsibilities, finding it hard to manage everyday challenges and effectively prioritize your time.

Identifying these signs is the first step towards recovery and growth. Seek help from loved ones or professionals to guide you towards healthier development. Remember, caring for others starts with self-care.

ENNEAGRAM TYPE 1: HEALTHY, AVERAGE, UNHEALTHY

As an Enneagram Type 1, you aim for perfection and have a strong desire to serve, striving to positively impact the world. In your healthy state, you display integrity, responsibility, and conscientiousness, committed to justice and purposeful tasks. You are a moral guide, continuously improving yourself and the world, excelling in precision and problem-solving.

However, in your average state, your quest for perfection may lead to rigidity, self-criticism, and a focus on flaws over achievements, leading to frustration if things veer off plan.

In your unhealthy state, your high standards may become unrealistic, leading to judgment, rigidity, anger, and potential conflicts due to imposing your views on others.

As an Enneagram Type 1, it's important to balance self-improvement with kindness and forgiveness. By accepting imperfections, you can serve with compassion and make a tangible difference.

ENNEAGRAM TYPE 2: HEALTHY, AVERAGE, UNHEALTHY

Enneagram Type 2 individuals are driven by a deep desire to help others and seek validation, and their behaviour varies across healthy, average, and unhealthy levels of development.

Healthy Type 2s are selfless and empathetic, able to set boundaries and express their needs while offering support to others. They have a strong self-worth, give without expectations, and receive with grace, fostering genuine relationships. Additionally, they prioritize self-care, understanding it enables them to better assist others.

Average Type 2s may struggle with setting boundaries, becoming overly involved in others' lives and neglecting their own needs. They often seek approval, leading to feelings of exhaustion and being undervalued. They may also resort to passive-aggressive behaviour to meet their needs.

Unhealthy Type 2s may become overly reliant on others for self-worth, sacrificing their well-being for validation. They may exhibit possessiveness and fear of abandonment, and may use their helpful nature to manipulate others.

As they develop, Type 2 individuals can learn to balance their service inclination with self-care, fostering healthier relationships and a stronger self-worth.

ENNEAGRAM TYPE 3: HEALTHY, AVERAGE, UNHEALTHY

Type 3 individuals exhibit behaviors guided by their desire for success and recognition, which varies with their level of development. In a healthy state, they use their talents to inspire others, balancing their aspirations with the needs of their surroundings. They are admired for their efficiency, hard work, and determination.

However, when average, their pursuit of success becomes self-centered, prioritizing their achievements over others' welfare. They seek validation, tend to lose authenticity, and present a fabricated image to the world, often becoming overly competitive.

In an unhealthy state, they may resort to manipulation and deceit to maintain their image and achieve their goals, leading to burnout. They may lose touch with their empathy, neglecting others' needs and feelings in their success pursuit.

For effective service, Type 3 individuals need to balance their ambitions and the well-being of others. They should embrace authenticity, value genuine connections over external validation, and direct their success drive towards meaningful goals, inspiring and uplifting others while achieving their own aspirations.

ENNEAGRAM TYPE 4: HEALTHY, AVERAGE, UNHEALTHY

Healthy Enneagram Type 4 individuals showcase their distinct creativity and emotional depth, inspiring their environment. Key traits of a healthy Type 4 include:

- **Deep self-awareness**: They possess a profound grasp of their inner world, including their feelings, desires, and motivations, which helps them live authentically and with integrity.
- **Emotional intelligence**: They are highly sensitive to their own and others' emotions, allowing them to empathize deeply and connect profoundly with others. Their ability to healthily express and process emotions can comfort and heal those around them.

- **Creative expression**: Their inherent creativity thrives in a healthy state, enabling them to express their deep emotions and experiences creatively and inspire others.
- **Appreciation for beauty**: They are aesthetically aware and appreciate beauty in all forms, finding comfort and inspiration in it. Their ability to identify and create beauty brings joy and inspiration to others.

In a healthy state, Enneagram Type 4 individuals inspire, comfort, and heal others by sharing their unique creativity, emotional depth, and authenticity.

ENNEAGRAM TYPE 5: HEALTHY, AVERAGE, UNHEALTHY

As a healthy Type 5, you possess extensive knowledge in your field, constantly seek new information, and can analyze and synthesize complex ideas to solve problems and provide unique viewpoints. You value teamwork, actively sharing your insights and offering mentorship to less experienced colleagues. You understand that empowering others can generate a broader positive impact.

You maintain a balanced work-life by taking breaks, nurturing personal relationships, and prioritizing self-care, ensuring sustained energy and enthusiasm for your work. The combination of your deep knowledge, team spirit, commitment to wellbeing, and desire to serve others defines you as a servant leader. Your dedication inspires and uplifts those working with you, making you an invaluable asset in your field.

ENNEAGRAM TYPE 6: HEALTHY, AVERAGE, UNHEALTHY

As an Enneagram Type 6, you naturally anticipate challenges and risks, making you an invaluable team member. Your traits contribute to the wellbeing of others and group stability. The key characteristics at various development levels include:

- Healthy Level: You're loyal to causes you trust, foresee potential issues and find solutions, support and protect team members, and create safety and stability by anticipating risks.
- Average Level: You may be overly anxious, seeking constant reassurance, and excessively skeptical. You may overly rely on rules and authority, and your loyalty may waver due to trust issues.
- Unhealthy Level: Overwhelming fear may lead to paranoia and distrust. You may impulsively seek safety and reassurance, become cynical, and undermine others. Your loyalty may transform into blind obedience or rebellion.

Understanding these levels can boost personal growth and your effectiveness. By balancing caution and trust, you can be a reliable, supportive presence in any team.

ENNEAGRAM TYPE 7: HEALTHY, AVERAGE, UNHEALTHY

Let's talk about the points of Enneagram Type 7's development. The healthy traits of a Type 7 include being adventurous, optimistic, and enthusiastic. However, when in an average state, Type 7 individuals tend to become scattered, restless, and constantly seeking new experiences. In an unhealthy state, Type 7s can become impulsive, reckless, and avoid dealing with their emotions.

Type 7's Healthy Traits

Healthy Type 7s in the Enneagram system have beneficial traits including optimism, creativity, adventurousness, and enthusiasm. They inspire hope by seeing life's positive aspects, solve problems uniquely due to their imaginative nature, foster growth by encouraging new experiences, and motivate others with their infectious enthusiasm. These traits allow them to effectively bring joy and adventure to their interactions.

Average Type 7 Behaviors

Average Type 7 behaviors encompass a constant desire for new experiences and distractions, a fear of missing out, and struggle to remain in the moment. It's vital for those wishing to serve others to identify these traits in themselves or others. Although pursuing new experiences is thrilling, it's important to strike a balance and avoid constant interruptions. The fear of missing out can instigate a relentless need for stimulation, leading to feelings of restlessness and dissatisfaction. Struggling to stay in the moment can hinder meaningful engagements and experiences. Recognizing these behaviors can aid in achieving a healthy balance and improving focus and presence in service to others.

Unhealthy Type 7 Traits

Unhealthy Type 7 traits include extreme impulsivity and an inability to focus, leading to task incompletion and a constant need for stimulation. Four main traits are escapism, restlessness, self-absorption, and a lack of self-discipline. Understanding these can help support Type 7 individuals struggling with them. By providing patience, guidance, and encouraging fear confrontation, you can aid them towards a healthier and more fulfilling path.

ENNEAGRAM TYPE 8: HEALTHY, AVERAGE, UNHEALTHY

This article explores the Enneagram Type 8's development levels, highlighting their healthy, average, and unhealthy behaviors. Healthy Type 8s demonstrate a strong sense of justice, defending the weak and standing against injustice with their power and authority. Their assertiveness, balanced with empathy and compassion, makes them inspiring leaders who promote fairness and are ready to make personal sacrifices.

In an average state, Type 8s can become controlling and prone to anger. Their assertiveness may escalate to dominance, and their drive for justice may turn aggressive.

They might disregard other's opinions, leading to strained relationships and mistrust.

At their worst, Type 8s can turn tyrannical and abusive, using their power for manipulation and coercion. Their behaviors, driven by fear of vulnerability, can escalate to bullying and aggression, causing harm.

Understanding these development levels can aid our interactions with Type 8s, encouraging their growth and using their leadership skills for greater good.

ENNEAGRAM TYPE 9: HEALTHY, AVERAGE, UNHEALTHY

Exploring Enneagram Type 9's development levels reveals their healthy, average, and unhealthy behaviors. They strive for inner peace, often avoiding conflict and empathizing with others. Key characteristics include:

- Healthy: They exude peace, are open-minded, value others' perspectives, and mediate well. They assert themselves when necessary, without ignoring their needs.
- Average: They often put others first, ignoring their needs and avoiding conflicts. They might indirectly express frustration, struggle with decision-making, and resist change, preferring the comfort of familiar routines.
- Unhealthy: They may disconnect emotionally, isolating themselves to steer clear of conflict. They might procrastinate and shirk

responsibilities, resulting in low productivity.
They can become stubborn and resistant to
change, clinging to a stagnant life.

Understanding these levels gives insight into Type 9's behaviors and motivations. Recognizing unhealthy patterns can spur growth and balance between their needs and those of others.

IDENTIFYING YOUR LEVEL OF DEVELOPMENT

To determine your Enneagram development level, scrutinize your behaviors, motivations, and reactions to challenges. This understanding can reveal areas for self-improvement. The Enneagram classifies development into three levels: healthy, average, and unhealthy. The healthy level signifies the peak of your personality type, characterized by self-awareness, balance, and ease in handling life's hurdles, with a focus on positively impacting others.

The average level is a blend of good and bad traits, often driven by a need for approval and fear of rejection. The unhealthy level is dominated by negative emotions like fear and anger, leading to manipulative, aggressive or withdrawn behavior. It's marked by a lack of self-awareness and self-centrism.

Assessing your behaviors and motivations honestly can provide insights into your development level. The aim is not self-judgment, but better self-understanding for personal growth.

TIPS FOR MOVING TOWARD HEALTH AND GROWTH

To move toward health and growth, start by recognizing negative patterns in your behavior and thought processes. Cultivate self-awareness by observing your actions, reactions, and emotions without judgment. Additionally, consider seeking professional guidance from a therapist or coach who can provide valuable insight and support on your journey towards personal development.

Recognizing Negative Patterns

1. Identifying and addressing negative behavioral patterns are crucial for personal growth and effective service to others. Here are some concise tips:

- Reflect on your actions: Spend time identifying recurring unproductive patterns in your behavior.
- Seek feedback: Get feedback from trusted acquaintances on how your behavior affects them for valuable insights.
- Practice mindfulness: Use mindfulness to non-judgmentally observe your thoughts, feelings, and actions, helping you recognize negative patterns and consciously modify them.

- Set attainable goals: Segment your personal growth journey into manageable goals to maintain motivation and monitor progress.

Cultivating Self-Awareness

Cultivate self-awareness for personal growth and improved service to others by reflecting on your actions and seeking feedback from trusted individuals. This process helps identify behavioral patterns and growth areas, as well as offering external perspectives on your persona. The feedback can reveal unnoticed areas of improvement. The ongoing process of self-awareness demands humility, open-mindedness, and a genuine wish to grow. Embrace the journey and use the insights to better yourself and serve others more effectively.

Seeking Professional Guidance

Begin your personal growth journey by consulting a qualified professional. Essential tips include finding a therapist or coach specializing in personal development and the Enneagram system, sharing your fears and goals openly for a personalized plan, maintaining regular sessions for consistent progress, and applying insights learned outside the sessions. Remember, investing in professional guidance can lead to desired health and growth with the right support.

FREQUENTLY ASKED QUESTIONS

How Can I Identify My Level of Development According to the Enneagram?

Let's talk about figuring out your Enneagram development level. It's pretty simple, actually. Just think about your actions, thoughts, and feelings. Check if there's a pattern in how you react to stress or arguments. Do you often react with kindness and understanding, or do you find yourself stuck in negative loops? Stay aware of yourself. This is the key to understand where you stand and how to grow. Keep it up!

What Are Some Common Characteristics of the Healthy Level of Development?

When you're at a healthy level of development, you start showing some really great qualities. You feel at peace with yourself, understand your feelings better, and keep them under control. On top of that, you naturally become kind, compassionate, and empathetic to others. This is an awesome stage because it helps you form strong bonds and positively influence people around you. Keep going, you're doing great!

Are There Any Specific Signs or Indicators of an Unhealthy Level of Development?

Feeling stuck or lost? It's possible that you're at an unhealthy stage in your life. If you notice you're always seeking approval or blaming others for your issues, pay attention. Struggling to take responsibility for yourself or constantly comparing yourself to others can also be signs. It's a wake-up call – it's time to work on you and progress towards a healthier stage in life.

Can You Provide Examples of Enneagram Types at Each Level of Development?

Absolutely! Let's dive right into the concept of Enneagram types across different development stages. Picture this - when you're in a healthy state, no matter your type, you tend to show good qualities and act in positive ways. Slip to an average state, and you might start to show some not-so-great habits or attitudes. Fall to an unhealthy state, and those negative traits might become even more intense and possibly damaging. Recognizing these levels can really give you a clear picture of where you stand on your own journey to personal growth. Keep pushing forward!

What Are Some Tips or Strategies for Moving Towards Health and Growth According to the Enneagram?

Let's talk about moving towards health and growth with the Enneagram. It's all about focusing on you. Understand what drives you and what scares you. Reflect on yourself and be ready for feedback. Set achievable goals that match your values and chase them. Be kind to yourself, learn to forgive your slip-ups. Find a supportive squad that cheers on your growth. This is your journey, so patience and kindness to yourself are key.

CONCLUSION

Wrapping up this chapter, getting to grips with the Enneagram levels of development can offer us some real gems for our personal growth and wellness. It's about figuring out where we stand right now, and then setting sights on a healthier, more rewarding life. It's like a caterpillar morphing into a butterfly, right? Embracing our potential for growth can spark a stunning, life-changing journey of self-discovery. So, ready to unfurl your wings and fly towards a sunnier future? Let's do it!

CHAPTER 9
GROWTH AND STRESS ARROWS

Think you've got yourself all figured out? Let's dive into a new perspective on your Enneagram type. In this chapter, we're exploring the powerful impact of growth and stress arrows on each personality type. From the quest for perfection for Type 1 to the bold journey of self-assertion for Type 9, we'll uncover how embracing growth and managing stress can lead you to a more fulfilling, balanced life. So, buckle up! It's time to unleash your potential and make a positive impact on those around you.

TYPE 1 GROWTH AND STRESS ARROWS

As a Type 1 individual, you grow and experience stress through your Enneagram integration and disintegration points. Your growth stems from adopting Type 7's positive attributes, such as spontaneity, joy, and open-mindedness, which can help you lessen your perfectionism and adopt a more lighthearted approach to life. This aids in serving others more freely and creatively. Conversely, stress leads you towards Type 4's negative traits, such as self-criticism, melancholy, and focusing on deficiencies. To avoid becoming too self-absorbed, it's crucial to consciously redirect your attention to positive aspects of yourself and your surroundings. Ultimately, by understanding these dynamics, you can maintain your integrity, compassion, and purpose in service to others.

TYPE 2 GROWTH AND STRESS ARROWS

As a Type 2 individual, your growth involves balancing self-care with your innate desire to serve others. Harnessing the positive traits of Type 4, such as emotional self-awareness, can enhance your understanding of personal motivations and help avoid overdependency on others' validation. However, be alert to potential pitfalls, such as Type 8's controlling behaviors under stress. Healthier coping mechanisms, like self-care and boundary-setting, can prevent burnout. Embrace your ability to serve others, but not at the expense of your well-being.

TYPE 3 GROWTH AND STRESS ARROWS

Now let's explore the growth patterns for Type 3 individuals. Understanding how Type 3s can develop and thrive will provide valuable insights into their personal and professional development. Additionally, we will discuss effective strategies for managing stress as a Type 3, as well as the specific Enneagram arrows that influence their behavior and mindset.

Type 3's Growth Patterns

As a Type 3, growth comes from embracing vulnerability and authenticity, understanding that your value isn't solely tied to achievements or others' opinions. Showing your true self can foster deeper, genuine relationships. This growth involves moving away from needing to prove yourself, and instead, focusing on creating meaningful connections. Authenticity is central to this, aligning your actions with your values. By adopting vulnerability and authenticity, you can achieve personal growth and satisfaction in serving others sincerely.

Managing Stress as Type 3

As a Type 3, stress management involves recognizing overworking tendencies and striving for perfection, while also prioritizing self-care for a balanced work-life. Understanding that continuous self-push can result in burnout is vital. Remember, breaks and self-care are essential for your well-being, not a weakness. Engage in joyful and relaxing activities such as spending time with loved ones or hobbies. Self-care not only improves your service to others but also reenergizes you for goal pursuit.

Enneagram Arrows for Type 3

Type 3 Enneagram's growth and stress responses are crucial to understand. Driven by the desire to succeed and appear successful, Type 3s, in growth, adopt positive qualities of Type 6, like loyalty, responsibility, and trust-worthiness, fostering deeper, trust-based relationships. However, during stress, they may display negative Type 9 traits like disconnection, passivity, and conflict avoidance. Recognizing these patterns and striving for balance and self-awareness can help them serve others authentically and with integrity.

TYPE 4 GROWTH AND STRESS ARROWS

Navigating Enneagram Type 4's growth and stress arrows involves embracing your uniqueness, cultivating self-compassion, seeking connection, and avoiding self-absorption.

1. Embrace your uniqueness: Your individuality is a gift that offers an artistic perspective to the world. Expressing yourself authentically and celebrating your distinct qualities fosters creativity and beauty.
2. Cultivate self-compassion: As a Type 4, you may experience self-doubt and criticism. It's crucial to practice self-compassion, acknowledging your emotions and embracing your sensitivity, promoting inner peace and self-nurturing.
3. Seek connection: While individuality is key, human connection is also vital for personal growth. Engage with those who share your interests and values, creating a supportive and appreciative environment that leads to a sense of belonging and fulfillment.

4. Avoid self-absorption: Beware of excessive self-absorption. Balance self-reflection with empathy for others' perspectives. Actively listen to those around you to foster understanding and harmonious relationships.

With self-awareness, self-compassion, and a willingness to connect, you can navigate Type 4's growth and stress arrows, leading to greater personal fulfillment and the opportunity to share your unique gifts with the world.

TYPE 5 GROWTH AND STRESS ARROWS

Type 5 individuals grow and manage stress by deepening their understanding and balancing solitude with meaningful relationships. As a Type 5, you flourish by gathering information and broadening your comprehension of your surroundings. In growth, you become more receptive and willing to share your knowledge, providing useful insights and solutions to others' issues.

For growth, stepping out of your comfort zone and engaging in social interactions is crucial. Solitude is essential for your personal renewal, but it's equally vital to forge meaningful connections. Doing so enriches your knowledge and understanding through others' experiences.

Under stress, you may retreat into solitude, leading to isolation and detachment, hindering your ability to serve others and becoming disconnected from your needs. To avoid this, recognize when you're overwhelmed, and proactively reach out to others. Seek help from trusted friends or mentors to navigate stress. By balancing solitude and meaningful connections, you can continue to expand intellectually while meaningfully serving others.

TYPE 6 GROWTH AND STRESS ARROWS

Now let's talk about the growth and stress arrows for Type 6. Type 6 individuals tend to respond to stress by becoming more cautious and seeking guidance from others. However, when they are able to manage stress effectively, they can develop a sense of inner strength and self-confidence. Understanding these response patterns can help Type 6 individuals navigate stressful situations and foster personal growth.

Type 6 Response Patterns

Enneagram Type 6 individuals may display four response patterns under stress or growth:

1. **Seeking Security**: They may become cautious, seeking others' reassurance and stability in relationships during stress.
2. **Increased Loyalty**: Challenges may enhance their loyalty and dedication to loved ones, with efforts to support and protect them for comfort and stability.
3. **Overthinking and Doubt**: Stress may induce excessive worry, doubt, and overanalysis, leading to constant self-questioning and validation-seeking.

4. **Embracing Courage**: Growth periods can foster inner strength, courage, increased self-assurance, instinct trust, and risk-taking to conquer fears.

Understanding these patterns aids Type 6 individuals in personal growth and healthy stress management.

Managing Stress Effectively

To manage stress effectively as a Type 6, cultivate personal growth and resilience strategies. Prioritize self-care, establish a strong support network for guidance, and use mindfulness techniques to stay present and lessen anxiety. Regular exercise, a balanced diet, and setting achievable goals also contribute to resilience. These strategies assist in stress management without compromising your desire to serve others.

TYPE 7 GROWTH AND STRESS ARROWS

Type 7 individuals on their Enneagram journey seek new experiences and shun discomfort. To help them grow, it's vital to understand their growth and stress arrows.

Type 7 Growth Arrows:

1. Embrace Limitations: Encourage Type 7s to confront fears and accept limitations, promoting growth through overcoming challenges.
2. Stay Present: Remind Type 7s to engage in the moment and appreciate stillness, without always seeking the next thrill.

3. Cultivate Patience: Assist Type 7s in building patience by slowing down and fully absorbing each experience, highlighting the drawbacks of instant gratification.

4. Develop Emotional Depth: Support Type 7s in expressing deeper emotions, promoting vulnerability and facing underlying discomfort.

Type 7 Stress Arrows:

1. Becoming Critical: Reassure Type 7s under stress to replace self-criticism with constructive feedback and self-compassion.

2. Seeking Constant Distraction: Encourage Type 7s to use healthy stress outlets like mindfulness or creativity instead of avoiding emotions.

3. Restlessness and Impulsivity: Guide Type 7s to manage restlessness and impulsivity under stress, prompting them to reflect and make mindful choices.

4. Fear of Missing Out: Remind stressed Type 7s that taking breaks and prioritizing self-care won't result in missing all new experiences.

TYPE 8 GROWTH AND STRESS ARROWS

Type 8's Enneagram journey involves specific growth and stress arrows. As a Type 8, your assertiveness is inherent but growth comes from developing vulnerability and becoming more receptive to others' needs.

During growth periods, you embody Type 2's positive traits, becoming more compassionate, nurturing, and service-oriented. This shift from self-reliance to building meaningful connections with others deepens your relationships.

In contrast, stress periods may lead you to display unhealthy Type 5 traits, like withdrawing and excessively defending your boundaries. Counteracting this with activities that pique your curiosity and foster learning can restore balance and strength.

To continue evolving as a Type 8, balancing your assertiveness and vulnerability is key. Acknowledging others' needs and accepting their support can lead to a more harmonious life. Serving others doesn't weaken you, but strengthens you. Face growth and stress with determination and self-awareness.

TYPE 9 GROWTH AND STRESS ARROWS

As a Type 9, growth periods require exploring new possibilities and prioritizing harmony in relationships. Here are four ways to achieve this:

1. **Embrace Conflict Resolution:** Tackle conflicts directly instead of avoiding them. Understand others' perspectives and find resolution common ground. This approach deepens connections and enhances harmony.
2. **Express Your Needs:** Recognize and communicate your needs and boundaries, which

are often overlooked in favor of others. Assertive yet respectful expression of your needs cultivates healthier, mutually respectful relationships.

3. **Take Initiative:** Challenge yourself to lead in various life areas. Initiating new projects, volunteering, or expressing your ideas in groups can boost confidence and positively impact others.

4. **Seek Self-Awareness:** Engage in self-reflection to understand your desires, values, and passions. This alignment with your authentic self helps make fulfilling choices that also benefit others effectively.

FREQUENTLY ASKED QUESTIONS

What Are the Key Characteristics and Behaviors of Type 1 Individuals in Their Growth and Stress States?

As a type 1 individual, when you're growing and evolving, you'll notice some positive traits. You'll become more open to different ideas, flexible in your approach, and ready to embrace change. You'll also start dropping that "everything needs to be perfect" attitude and learn to forgive yourself and others more easily.

But, when you're stressed, things might take a different turn. You might find yourself becoming more critical, stickler for rules, and judgmental. Feelings of frustration might fill you and controlling situations might become your way to feel stable again. Remember, it's okay to experience these emotions. The key is to acknowledge them and work towards managing them effectively. You've got this!

How Do Type 2 Individuals Typically Respond to Growth and Stress Situations?

When it comes to growth and stress, type 2 people usually react by stepping up to help others. When you're growing, you might notice you're becoming more aware of yourself and setting healthier boundaries. This can make you feel more independent and capable. But be careful during stressful times, as you might focus too much on helping others and forget to take care of yourself.

What Are Some Common Signs of Growth and Stress for Type 3 Individuals?

Let's talk about some typical signs of growth and stress for a type 3 personality like you. When you're growing, you tend to aim for success and recognition - you're more focused, self-assured, and goal-oriented. On the flip side, stress can make you overly competitive, impatient, and even a workaholic. It's crucial to balance your drive with self-care, and always remember, you're more than just your achievements.

How Do Type 4 Individuals Tend to Experience Growth and Stress Arrows?

People who fall under Type 4, here's what you need to know. When you're growing, you become tougher, more flexible, and open to new things. It's your chance to discover yourself, to bloom in your creativity and originality. But when stress hits, you might pull back and become moody, overwhelmed by your feelings and desiring a deeper connection. Recognize these patterns and find healthy ways to deal with them. You've got this!

Can You Provide Examples of How Type 5 Individuals May Behave When They Are in a Growth or Stress State?

If you're a type 5 individual, here's how you might act when you're growing or feeling stressed. When things are going well, you could find yourself being more open and ready to connect with people. You might also feel more self-assured and eager to tackle new challenges. But if you're stressed, you might pull back a bit, feeling more alone and disconnected from others. You could also feel more anxious and overwhelmed by what's being asked of you. Keep going, you're doing great!

CONCLUSION

Wrapping up this chapter, getting a grip on the growth and stress arrows of each enneagram type can shed some light on our personal growth journey. Spotting these behavior patterns when we're thriving or under pressure allows us to handle these situations with a clear mind. So, isn't it exciting to use these tough times as stepping stones for personal growth and learning?

CHAPTER 10
CORE BELIEFS AND PATTERNS

Intrigued about the core beliefs and patterns of different enneagram types? Let's take a fascinating journey together into the unique world that shapes each type. From the perfectionists with a critical edge who identify as Type 1, to the people-pleasers who often put others before themselves as Type 2, this chapter will shed light on the distinct traits of each enneagram type. You'll see how these patterns play a role in your relationships, behavior, and personal growth. Plus, we'll dive into the ways to better understand and serve others. So, ready for this insightful exploration?

TYPE 1: PERFECTIONISTIC AND CRITICAL PATTERNS

As a Type 1 in the Enneagram system, your perfectionistic and critical tendencies shape your thoughts and actions. You aim to serve and improve the world, but your quest for perfection can hinder your effectiveness.

This desire for perfection roots from your belief of worthiness equating to being flawless. Having high personal and external standards, you may judge yourself and others harshly for not meeting them, creating stress in your relationships.

In your pursuit of perfection, you become overly critical of yourself, leading to self-doubt. Remember that perfection is unattainable and mistakes are inevitable. To combat these tendencies, practice self-compassion and acceptance, be more forgiving towards yourself and others, and understand that errors are natural. Concentrate on progress instead of perfection and appreciate your accomplishments, irrespective of their size.

TYPE 2: PEOPLE-PLEASING AND SELF-SACRIFICING PATTERNS

Type 2 individuals in the Enneagram system display people-pleasing and self-sacrificing behaviors, driven by a desire to be loved and needed. They prioritize others' needs over their own, believing their worth is determined by their ability to help others. They anticipate and fulfill others' needs, seeking validation from being helpful. However, this can result in neglecting their own needs and desires.

Their self-sacrifice aligns with their people-pleasing nature, often ignoring their own feelings to prioritize others' well-being. While commendable, this can lead to resentment and burnout without self-care.

It's crucial for Type 2 individuals to understand that their worth isn't solely linked to their service to others. They should set boundaries, prioritize self-care, and seek help when needed, to maintain a balanced approach. They are just as deserving of love and care as those they serve.

TYPE 3: ACHIEVER AND IMAGE-ORIENTED PATTERNS

As Type 2 individuals evolve into Type 3 or the Achiever, they adopt an image-conscious and success-driven mindset. They believe their value is tied to their accomplishments and the image they project. They are highly ambitious, constantly striving for success, and are often seen as confident and charismatic leaders.

Image perception is critical to Type 3s; they work diligently to maintain a positive image, skillfully presenting themselves in an appealing manner. However, their pursuit of success and admiration may cause them to lose touch with their authentic selves and values, potentially leading to dissatisfaction since their self-worth relies on external validation.

In essence, the transition from Type 2 to Type 3 involves adopting a goal-oriented and image-conscious mindset. It's important for Type 3s to balance their ambition with self-awareness, ensuring they stay true to their authentic selves.

TYPE 4: INDIVIDUALISTIC AND EMOTIONALLY INTENSE PATTERNS

Type 4 individuals are characterized by a strong sense of individuality and intense emotional experiences. Their belief in their distinctiveness guides their actions. Core to Type 4 is the notion that they lack something others possess, leading to envy and a persistent search for completeness.

They experience a broad spectrum of deeply felt emotions, which they can express creatively, inspiring their artistic pursuits. However, they can also grapple with feelings of melancholy and isolation. Yet, their unique outlook allows them to appreciate the beauty in normality and find significance in the everyday.

As Type 4, their emotional depth connects them with others' feelings, making them empathetic listeners and a comforting presence. Their uniqueness and emotional connection equip them to assist others in their emotional exploration. In essence, Type 4's individuality and emotional intensity shape their world view and enable them to provide emotional support to others.

TYPE 5: OBSERVER AND DETACHED PATTERNS

Type 5 individuals are detached and observant, analyzing and learning from afar. Recognizing their patterns is key for productive interactions, given their propensity for detachment. Two key insights into Type 5s include:

- **Loneliness and Isolation:** They often withdraw socially, valuing solitude and autonomy. This can result in feelings of loneliness and isolation. It's crucial to approach Type 5s with empathy, offering them a sense of connection.
- **Fear of Inadequacy:** They may fear not having enough knowledge or resources, leading them to continuously seek information. Offering reassurance and support can help them overcome their fear and reach their potential.

Understanding Type 5s' detached nature allows sensitive and compassionate interactions. Acknowledging their need for space and addressing their fears creates an environment where they feel seen and supported. Serving others means meeting them where they are - respecting Type 5s' need for distance, while providing connection and reassurance.

TYPE 6: LOYALIST

Type Sixes in the Enneagram system, also known as The Loyalist, are typically motivated by a need for security and support, and they have a strong focus on problems and potential hazards as a way of preparing and protecting themselves and others.

Core Beliefs:

- There is danger in the world, and I must be prepared.

- I can't fully trust myself or others; it's important to question everything.

- Consistency, reliability, and loyalty are paramount.

Behavioral Patterns:

- Tendency to worry and imagine worst-case scenarios.

- Seeking reassurance and validation from others.

- Alertness to danger and potential problems.

- Strong sense of duty and responsibility.

- Often committed, hard-working, and trustworthy.

Remember, these are general traits and may not apply to every individual who identifies as a Type Six. The Enneagram is a tool for understanding human behavior and should not be used to stereotype or box people into rigid categories.

TYPE 7: ENTHUSIAST

Type Sevens in the Enneagram system, also known as The Enthusiast, are typically motivated by a need for freedom, adventure, and excitement. They seek to avoid pain and boredom by focusing on positive possibilities and options.

Core Beliefs:

• Life is an adventure full of exciting possibilities.

- It's important to avoid pain, discomfort, and boredom.
- Satisfaction and happiness come from new experiences.

Behavioral Patterns:

- Tendency to plan and anticipate future adventures and possibilities.
- Difficulty dealing with negative feelings or boredom, often avoiding them by staying busy.
- Strive for a life full of varied experiences and enjoy exploring.
- Often enthusiastic, optimistic, and energetic.
- Can struggle with impulsivity and may have difficulty committing.

Again, these are general traits and may not fully describe every individual who identifies as a Type Seven. The Enneagram is a holistic system that accounts for individual variations and should not be used to stereotype or categorize people strictly.

TYPE 8: CHALLENGER

Type Eights in the Enneagram system, also known as The Challenger, are typically motivated by a need to be self-reliant, strong, and avoid showing vulnerability. They strive to protect themselves and those in their circle.

Core Beliefs:

- I must protect myself and those close to me.

- It's important to be strong and in control of my situation.

- Vulnerability is a weakness that can be exploited.

Behavioral Patterns:

- Tendency to confront or challenge what they perceive as injustices or wrongdoings.

- Often assertive, decisive, and willing to take the lead.

- May struggle with temper and impulsiveness, and can be perceived as intimidating.

- Tendency to deny their own vulnerability or needs for comfort and affection.

- Often value honesty and directness, even if it might seem too blunt for others.

As always, these are general traits and may not fully describe every individual who identifies as a Type Eight. The Enneagram is a tool for understanding complex human behavior and should not be used to stereotype or categorize people rigidly.

TYPE 9: PEACEMAKER

Type Nines in the Enneagram system, also known as The Peacemaker, are typically motivated by a desire for inner and outer peace, comfort, and to avoid conflict. They often struggle with inertia and inaction due to their desire to maintain the status quo.

Core Beliefs:

- Peace and harmony are essential.

- It's best to avoid conflict and tension.

- My needs and desires aren't as important as keeping peace and comfort.

Behavioral Patterns:

- Tendency to go along with others to keep the peace, even at the cost of their own needs or desires.

- Struggle with inertia and inaction; can be perceived as complacent or stubborn.

- Often have a calming and grounding influence on others.

- May avoid or dismiss problems in hopes they will go away on their own.

- Tendency to disengage from stressful situations to seek comfort and tranquility.

Remember, these are general traits and may not fully encapsulate the behavior of every individual who identifies as a Type Nine. The Enneagram is a holistic system that considers individual variations and should not be used to stereotype or rigidly categorize people.

FREQUENTLY ASKED QUESTIONS

How Do Enneagram Type 1 Individuals Handle Criticism From Others?

Handling criticism can be tough, right? But for you as a Type 1 on the Enneagram, it can be a golden chance to grow. Next time you face criticism, don't rush to defend yourself. Pause for a moment. Is there some truth in it? Instead of raising your guard, keep an open mind and be ready to learn and get better. It's all about turning a challenge into an opportunity!

Are Enneagram Type 2 Individuals Always Overly Self-Sacrificing in Their Relationships?

Do you wonder if enneagram type 2 individuals are always overly self-sacrificing in their relationships? These folks are truly selfless. They go the extra mile to make others happy, often putting their own needs aside. It's as if they're wearing a superhero cape, always on standby to lend a hand. But remember, self-care is just as important, even if your goal is to make others happy.

What Are Some Common Struggles That Enneagram Type 3 Individuals Face When It Comes to Maintaining Their Image?

If you're an Enneagram Type 3, maintaining your image might be a little tough at times. You might feel like you constantly have to show off your successes to get approval from others. Being scared of failure might also be a problem because it could shatter your perfect image.

But remember, balancing the need for praise with staying true to yourself can be tough, but it's crucial for your own growth and happiness. So, keep going, you're doing great!

How Do Enneagram Type 4 Individuals Express Their Individuality in Their Daily Lives?

People who identify as Enneagram Type 4 have a knack for showing their uniqueness in their daily life. They have this strong urge to be genuine and distinctive, which often drives them to engage in creative activities like art, music, or fashion. They boldly wear their emotions on their sleeves, unafraid to reveal their true selves to everyone around them. Their way of expressing their uniqueness is a powerful reminder for us all to celebrate our own individuality and live our lives authentically.

What Are Some Ways Enneagram Type 5 Individuals Can Overcome Their Tendency to Detach From Their Emotions and Relationships?

If you're a Type 5, you might often find yourself pulling away from your emotions and relationships. This isn't great for you in the long run, trust me. So, what can you do to change this? First, acknowledge your emotions - yes, even those big, scary ones. Try sharing your feelings in a place where you feel safe and supported. This could be with a close friend, or in therapy or support groups. Get involved in activities that help you connect emotionally with others. And don't forget to really listen and empathize when others are sharing with you. I know it sounds tough, but by embracing your vulnerability, you'll be able to form deeper and more meaningful relationships. You've got this!

CONCLUSION

Wrapping up this chapter, getting to grips with the core beliefs and patterns of each enneagram type is like having a secret insight into how people tick. Think of it like a symphony – each enneagram type is a different instrument, bringing their unique sound to the mix. The more we understand these different perspectives, the better we can connect with others. We're not just talking about improving relationships here, but making the world a more tolerant place.

CHAPTER 11
COMMON MISTYPINGS AND MISIDENTIFICATIONS

Stumped about your Enneagram type? You're not the only one. It's easy to stumble upon common mistakes and end up confused. But, don't worry! In this chapter, we're going to shed light on the most common mix-ups for each Enneagram type. By steering clear of these pitfalls, you'll be on your way to discovering your true type. Plus, you'll gain a deeper understanding of yourself and others. Ready to unravel the Enneagram mysteries? Let's jump in!

TYPE 1: COMMON MISTYPINGS AND MISIDENTIFICATIONS

When determining your Enneagram type, be mindful of common mistypings, particularly with Type 1, 'The Perfectionist.' It's crucial to distinguish genuine Type 1 characteristics from other types exhibiting similar traits.

It's easy to confuse Type 1 with Type 6, 'The Loyalist,' as both are responsible and conscientious. However, Type 6 is driven by security and loyalty, while Type 1 seeks perfection.

Misidentifying a Type 1 as a Type 3, 'The Achiever,' is another common error. Both are goal-driven and hard-working, but Type 3 seeks recognition, whereas Type 1 aims to bring order and integrity.

Avoid mistyping Type 1 as Type 8, 'The Challenger,' or Type 9, 'The Peacemaker.' These types can be assertive, but Type 1 focuses on improvement, Type 8 on control, and Type 9 on peace.

Understanding these mistypings will help clarify your Enneagram type and enhance your self-understanding. An accurate Enneagram type is key for personal growth and effective service to others.

TYPE 2: COMMON MISTYPINGS AND MISIDENTIFICATIONS

When it comes to Type 2 misidentifications and common mistypings, it's important to understand the key characteristics of this type. Type 2 individuals are often mistaken for Type 9s due to their desire for harmony and their tendency to prioritize the needs of others. They may also be misidentified as Type 6s because of their loyalty and their fear of rejection.

Type 2 Misidentifications

Type 2s on the Enneagram are often misidentified as Type 9 or 6 due to shared characteristics. This includes a tendency to prioritize others' needs, a nurturing disposition, a fear of rejection, and a desire for approval, which are also associated with Type 9's peace-seeking and Type 6's loyalty. However, each type has distinct motivations. Recognizing your unique traits can help confirm your true Enneagram type.

Common Mistypings for Type 2

Type 2s are often misidentified as Type 9 or 6 due to shared characteristics like serving others. However, Type 2s focus on meeting others' needs, often neglecting their own, unlike Type 9s who avoid conflict. Unlike Type 6s who value loyalty and security, Type 2s prioritize relationships and seek validation through assistance. Recognizing these differences can help Type 2s accurately identify their true nature.

TYPE 3: COMMON MISTYPINGS AND MISIDENTIFICATIONS

When trying to identify a Type 3, it's important not to mistake their driven nature for narcissism. While they may be highly ambitious and achievement-oriented, they are not necessarily self-centered or attention-seeking. Another common misinterpretation is confusing their adaptability with deceitfulness. Type 3s are skilled at adapting to different situations and personas, but this does not mean they are being deceptive or inauthentic.

Misinterpreting Driven as Narcissistic

Driven Type 3 individuals may seem narcissistic due to their ambitious nature, but their motivation actually stems from a desire for validation and approval. Key differences between Type 3s and narcissists include:

- **Motivation**: Type 3s aim for success and accomplishment, whereas narcissists crave admiration without necessarily achieving anything.
- **Empathy**: Type 3s can empathize and value others' opinions, unlike narcissists who often disregard others' needs.
- **Self-Reflection**: Type 3s willingly self-reflect and grow, while narcissists reject criticism and ignore their shortcomings.
- **Relationships**: Type 3s prioritize and maintain positive relationships, unlike narcissists who may use others for personal benefit and lack real emotional ties.

Recognizing these differences can prevent misinterpretation of a Type 3's ambition as narcissism, and promote an understanding of their need to serve and succeed.

Confusing Adaptability With Deceit

Continuing our discussion, it's essential to differentiate between adaptability and deceit in Type 3 individuals. These individuals are highly adaptable, adjusting their behavior, appearance, and goals to suit different situations. This adaptability, however, isn't equivalent to deceit. While they aim to present themselves optimally to reach their goals, their actions aren't driven by a desire to deceive or manipulate. Their adaptability is rooted in a need for success and recognition. Thus, in assessing Type 3 individuals, it's important to discern between their true adaptability and any perceived deceit.

TYPE 4: COMMON MISTYPINGS AND MISIDENTIFICATIONS

Many people often confuse Enneagram Type 4, also known as the Individualist or Romantic, with other types due to certain misconceptions. To understand Type 4's true essence, it's crucial to clear these misconceptions.

Common misidentifications of Type 4 include:

- Confusion with Type 2 (Helper or Giver): Both share emotional intensity, but Type 2 is more focused on others' needs, while Type 4 explores their own emotions and desires.
- Misinterpretation as Type 7 (Enthusiast or Adventurer): Both share enthusiasm and desire for new experiences, but Type 4 seeks authenticity and depth, while Type 7 avoids pain or discomfort.
- Confusion with Type 9 (Peacemaker or Mediator): Both desire harmony and avoid conflict, but Type 9 merges with others and

suppresses their desires, while Type 4 values
uniqueness and individuality.

- Mislabeling as Type 5 (Investigator or Observer):
  Both are introspective and desire knowledge, but
  Type 5 seeks understanding, while Type 4
  explores emotions and identity.

Understanding these misidentifications allows us to better comprehend Type 4's nature and effectively support individuals of this type, helping them embrace their authenticity and uniqueness.

TYPE 5: COMMON MISTYPINGS AND MISIDENTIFICATIONS

Type 5, or the Investigator, is frequently misidentified due to misconceptions about their personality traits. Understanding these can help serve their needs more effectively.

A common mistake is to mistake Type 5 for Type 6, the Loyalist. Despite both being analytical, Type 5s tend to withdraw to pursue intellectual interests and value independence, while Type 6s seek reassurance and rely on others for guidance.

Type 5 is also often confused with Type 9, the Peacemaker. Both can be reserved, but Type 5s strive for knowledge and expertise, while Type 9s seek inner peace, avoiding conflict to maintain unity.

Finally, Type 5 can be mistaken for Type 1, the Perfectionist. Both types are detail-oriented with a strong moral compass, but Type 5s are fueled by a thirst for knowledge while Type 1s aim for perfection and improvement.

Recognizing these misidentifications is crucial for accurately identifying and supporting Type 5 individuals, aiding their need for independence, intellectual stimulation, and deep understanding of their surroundings.

TYPE 6: COMMON MISTYPINGS AND MISIDENTIFICATIONS

Discussing common mistypings and misidentifications of Type 6 or 'The Loyalist' in the Enneagram system, we see these individuals are often misidentified due to certain characteristics. Here are some typical mistypings:

- Type 2: The Helper - Type 6's caring nature can lead to confusion with Type 2. However, Type 6's drive for security and skepticism differentiate them from Type 2.
- Type 9: The Peacemaker - Type 6's desire for peace can lead to misidentification as Type 9. Yet, Type 6 tends to seek security more actively and is often more anxious than Type 9.
- Type 1: The Perfectionist - Type 6's adherence to rules can resemble Type 1, but their need for security and propensity for anxiety marks them as different.

- Type 5: The Investigator - Type 6 shares a thirst for knowledge with Type 5, but their focus on security and skepticism sets them apart.

Recognizing these common mistypings helps ensure accurate self-assessment and better understanding of oneself and others. The Enneagram should be used as a tool for personal growth, approached with curiosity, empathy, and a service mindset.

TYPE 7: COMMON MISTYPINGS AND MISIDENTIFICATIONS

Are you having trouble determining whether you are a Type 7 in the Enneagram system? It's common for people to confuse Type 7 with other personalities, especially those with similar traits such as Type 3 or Type 9. Understanding the key differences and nuances between these types can help you avoid misidentifying yourself and gain a clearer understanding of your true Enneagram type.

Type 7 Confusion

Misidentifying Enneagram Type 7 is common due to its adventurous, enthusiastic nature, often mistaken for other types. Here are key distinctions to correctly identify Type 7:

- Fear of being trapped drives Type 7s, unlike Type 2s who fear being unloved.

- Unlike Type 4s who delve into their emotions, Type 7s avoid negativity by focusing on positive experiences.
- Type 7s, more future-oriented, don't dwell on the past like Type 6s who use past experiences for security.
- Unlike Type 9s who seek inner peace, Type 7s pursue external stimulation and novelty.

Understanding these distinctions will help determine if Type 7 is your true Enneagram type.

Common Mistyped Personalities

Enneagram Type 7 personalities are often misidentified due to their adventurous and enthusiastic traits, leading to confusion with Type 4 (the Individualist) or Type 3 (the Achiever). Both Type 7 and 4 share creativity and self-expression, but differ in motivations - Type 7 avoids discomfort seeking new experiences, while Type 4 values emotional depth striving for authenticity. Type 7 may also be confused with Type 3 due to shared high energy and success drive, but Type 7 aims to evade boredom, while Type 3 seeks recognition and external validation. Recognizing these nuances aids in correctly identifying Type 7 personalities.

Misidentifying Enneagram Type 7

Misidentifying Enneagram Type 7s can result from not recognizing their unique motivations and traits. They have a core desire for excitement and pain avoidance. Common misidentifications include:

- Type 7 vs. Type 3: Both may be outgoing and ambitious, but Type 7s seek new experiences, while Type 3s aim for success.
- Type 7 vs. Type 9: Type 7s desire stimulation and diversity, while Type 9s value peace and harmony.
- Type 7 vs. Type 1: Both may strive for perfection, but Type 7s emphasize positivity and may struggle with commitment, while Type 1s are guided by moral principles.
- Type 7 vs. Type 6: While Type 7s avoid discomfort and uncertainty, Type 6s crave security and tend to be cautious.

Recognizing these differences enhances the identification and support of Type 7 individuals, promoting balance and fulfillment in their lives.

TYPE 8: COMMON MISTYPINGS AND MISIDENTIFICATIONS

In identifying your Enneagram Type 8, be aware of the common misidentifications. Knowing your personality type accurately aids in effectively serving others.

Type 8 is often mistaken for Type 1, the Perfectionist. Both are assertive, but Type 1s strive for perfection and are self-critical, while Type 8s seek control and can be confrontational. Recognizing their different motivations is key.

Type 8 can also be confused with Type 3, the Achiever. Both are ambitious, but Type 8s aim for control and are direct, while Type 3s seek success and are more image-conscious. Understanding these motivations is crucial for accurate identification.

Some may misidentify as Type 8 when they are Type 6, the Loyalist. Both can be assertive, but Type 8s desire control, whereas Type 6s strive for security and tend to be more anxious. Distinguishing these motivations is essential.

Understanding these misidentifications can help you accurately identify your type, enhancing your self-awareness and ability to serve others effectively.

TYPE 9: COMMON MISTYPINGS AND MISIDENTIFICATIONS

Common mistypings for Enneagram Type 9 include Type 6, 2, 4, and 1. Type 9s may be mistaken for Type 6 due to shared conflict avoidance and need for security, but Type 6s are more anxious while Type 9s are generally more easygoing. Similarly, Type 9s may be misidentified as Type 2 for their shared value of harmony, but Type 2s seek to please others while Type 9s prioritize inner peace. Being mislabeled as Type 4 can occur due to a shared focus on emotions, but Type 4s embrace their uniqueness while Type 9s tend to merge with others. Lastly, Type 9s can be misidentified as Type 1 due to a shared value for integrity, but Type 1s have a critical inner voice and strive for perfection, unlike Type 9s. Accurate self-reflection is crucial to identify your true Enneagram type.

COMMON MISTYPINGS AND MISIDENTIFICATIONS OF THE ENNEAGRAM TYPES

Understanding the Enneagram types accurately requires recognizing and avoiding typical mistypings and misidentifications. It's easy to confuse Type 2, the Helper, with Type 9, the Peacemaker, due to their shared kindness and service-oriented nature. However, Type 2s need to be needed, whereas Type 9s aim for inner peace and conflict avoidance.

Similarly, Type 3, the Achiever, and Type 7, the Enthusiast, both energetic and driven, often get misidentified. Type 3s seek success and societal acceptance, while Type 7s fear missing out and aim to evade pain through new experiences.

Lastly, Type 5, the Investigator, and Type 6, the Loyalist, both analytical thinkers, are commonly mistaken for each other. Type 5s isolate to save energy and gain knowledge, while Type 6s lean on trusted relationships for security.

Being aware of these common mistakes can help you use the Enneagram accurately for self-awareness and personal growth.

TIPS FOR ACCURATE ENNEAGRAM TYPING AND IDENTIFICATION

To correctly identify your Enneagram type, observe key traits and behaviors. The Enneagram offers insights into your motives, fears, and wishes, aiding in self-discovery and growth. Here's how to determine your type:

- Examine your core motivations: Dig into your deepest fears and desires to understand what drives you. This could indicate your Enneagram type.
- Watch your behavior: Observe your reactions and interactions, noting if you seek security or chase new experiences. This could hint at your Enneagram type.
- Reflect on your childhood: Early experiences shape us. Consider how your upbringing has influenced your personality and coping strategies, further indicating your Enneagram type.
- Get external viewpoints: Feedback from trusted contacts or professionals can offer an objective view of your traits and behaviors.

FREQUENTLY ASKED QUESTIONS

Can I Be a Type 1 if I Don't Have a Strong Sense of Perfectionism or Desire for Control?

Absolutely, you can be a type 1 without a strong streak of perfectionism or control. Sure, these traits are often linked with type 1s, but remember, we're all unique and we might show different aspects of our type. Perfectionism and control aren't must-haves to be a type 1. Instead, try to grasp the key motivations and fears of a type 1 and see if they resonate with you. You got this!

How Can I Differentiate Between Type 2 and Type 6 if I Am a Caring and Helpful Person?

I understand that it might be tricky for you to tell the difference between type 2 and type 6, especially if you're someone who's naturally caring and helpful. But don't worry, I've got a straightforward way for you. It's all about what motivates you. If you find yourself driven by the need to feel needed and appreciated, you're likely a type 2. Now, if you're more about seeking security and support, you're probably leaning towards type 6. And, here's another tip: type 2s often focus more on others, while type 6s tend to zero in on their own worries and uncertainties. So, take a moment, think about it, and you'll figure it out. You got this!

Is It Possible for a Type 3 to Not Prioritize External Validation and Success?

Absolutely, a type 3 can choose not to focus on external validation and success. We're all unique, with different priorities, even within our Enneagram type. The Enneagram is just a guide for self-awareness and personal growth, not a box to confine yourself in. So, understand your motivations and desires, instead of worrying about fitting into a certain box. Trust yourself and forge your own path. You've got this!

Can a Type 4 Also Be Outgoing and Extraverted, or Are They Always Introverted and Melancholic?

Absolutely, a type 4 can be outgoing and extraverted! They aren't just introverted or melancholic. Enneagram types aren't trapped in certain personality traits. Type 4s can love socializing and enjoy expressing themselves in an extraverted way. Keep in mind, the Enneagram is a tool to help you discover yourself and everyone's journey is different. Celebrate your unique self, no matter your Enneagram type.

How Do I Know if I Am a Type 5 or a Type 9 if I Value Both Knowledge and Maintaining Peace?

Deciding if you're a type 5 or type 9, when you love both knowledge and peace, can be tricky. Let's make it simple. Think about how you act under stress. Do you pull away and dive into books or research? That's a classic type 5 response. Or do you dodge arguments and focus on keeping things calm? That's more a type 9 behavior. Reflecting on your stress responses may help you discover your true Enneagram type. Give it a shot!

CONCLUSION

So, you're wrapping up this chapter on common Enneagram mistypings and misidentifications. It's crucial to remember that figuring out your Enneagram type isn't a race. It's a journey of self-discovery that can be mind-opening. The Enneagram, with its intricate design, requires you to take some time to introspect. Don't just slap a label on yourself. Remember that timeless advice, 'Know thyself.' Dive deep into understanding your own fears, motivations, and desires. You'll find the Enneagram can be a game-changing tool for personal growth. Keep that in mind as you continue your journey.

CHAPTER 12

HOW TO ACCURATELY TYPE YOURSELF AND OTHERS

R eady to get to know yourself and those around you on a whole new level? Let's dive right into the fascinating world of the Enneagram system. It's a unique tool that helps you understand not just yourself, but others as well.

By exploring the nine Enneagram types, you'll start to see motivations, fears, and behavior patterns in a new light. You'll get to know yourself better and understand why people act the way they do.

With insights from Enneagram experts and feedback from others, you'll find opportunities for personal growth and build stronger connections. So, let's start this journey and learn to use the Enneagram to better serve others. Exciting, isn't it? This chapter is all about understanding and typing accurately on the Enneagram.

UNDERSTANDING THE ENNEAGRAM SYSTEM

The Enneagram system involves nine core personality types, each offering a unique perspective on our motives, fears, and desires. Type One, the Perfectionist or Reformer, is driven by a sense of responsibility and integrity, often striving for improvement and perfection, while Type Two, the Helper or Giver, is empathetic and nurturing, prioritizing the needs of others, sometimes to their own detriment. Type Three, the Achiever or Performer, is ambitious and goal-driven, seeking success and recognition, but can lose touch with their authentic selves in pursuit of external validation. Understanding these core personality types fosters empathy and compassion for oneself and others.

IMPORTANCE OF SELF-REFLECTION IN TYPING

Self-reflection is crucial for accurate Enneagram typing of oneself and others. It involves deep exploration of one's thoughts, emotions, and behaviors, helping to reveal unconscious patterns and motivations that influence actions. This process not only enhances self-awareness of one's fears, desires, defense mechanisms, strengths, and weaknesses, but it also clarifies core values and key motivations.

Moreover, self-reflection fosters empathy, allowing one to accurately type others on the Enneagram by picking up on subtle behavioral cues. However, it's key to approach this with humility and compassion due to individual uniqueness.

EXPLORING THE NINE ENNEAGRAM TYPES

Understanding the nine Enneagram types aids in self-identification and better serving others. Here's a brief overview:

- Type 1: The Perfectionist - Motivated by righteousness and ethics, they strive for perfection, are responsible, organized, principled, and self-critical.
- Type 2: The Helper - Driven by the need for love and necessity, they are warm, compassionate, supportive but may struggle to set boundaries.
- Type 3: The Achiever - Desires success, recognition, and admiration. They are goal-driven, adaptable but may seek too much external validation.
- Type 4: The Individualist - Seeks uniqueness and authenticity. They are emotionally sensitive, introspective, creative but may feel misunderstood.
- Type 5: The Investigator - Driven by understanding and knowledge, they are analytical, observant, independent but can become socially withdrawn.

- Type 6: The Loyalist - Desires security and guidance. They are dependable, loyal, responsible but may display anxiety.
- Type 7: The Enthusiast - Fears missing out; desires new experiences. They are energetic, spontaneous, and optimistic but can be impulsive.
- Type 8: The Challenger - Needs to be strong and in control. They are assertive, confident, protective but can struggle with vulnerability and authority.
- Type 9: The Peacemaker - Seeks inner and outer peace. They are easygoing, accommodating, supportive but may avoid conflict.

Understanding these traits helps meet unique needs and understand perspectives. Remember, individuals may display multiple types; approach with empathy and open-mindedness.

IDENTIFYING KEY MOTIVATIONS AND FEARS

Identifying each Enneagram type's fundamental motivations and fears aids in accurate self-typing and understanding of others. The Enneagram promotes personal growth and self-awareness, enhancing relationships through understanding these elements.

Type One, or the Perfectionist, desires to be good and fears immorality and mistakes. Type Twos, the Helpers, seek love and appreciation and fear being unwanted. Type Threes, the Achievers, long for success and admiration and fear failure and worthlessness.

Type Fours, the Individualists, yearn for uniqueness, fearing ordinariness and identity loss. Type Fives, the Investigators, need knowledge and understanding, fearing incapacity and overwhelming situations. Type Sixes, the Loyalists, desire security and support and fear abandonment and lack of guidance.

Type Sevens, the Enthusiasts, want excitement and fulfillment, fearing deprivation and pain. Type Eights, the Challengers, seek control and protection, fearing vulnerability and being controlled. Type Nines, the Peacemakers, long for peace and fear conflict and disconnection.

Understanding these core motivations and fears allows deeper insight into oneself and others. The Enneagram encourages growth, understanding, and compassion, enabling the formation of stronger, more meaningful relationships.

RECOGNIZING BEHAVIORAL PATTERNS AND TENDENCIES

To correctly identify Enneagram types, observe consistent behavioral patterns and inclinations. This can offer insights into personality types, motivations, and fears. Key patterns to consider include:

- **Reactive vs. Proactive:** Observe how people respond to situations. Reactive types tend to act on emotions impulsively, whereas proactive types consider consequences before acting.
- **Communication Style:** Note how people express themselves. Some may be assertive, others passive. Their preferred style can hint at their Enneagram type.
- **Problem-Solving Approach:** Pay attention to how people solve problems. Some prefer immediate solutions, while others analyze and gather information first. Their approach can give clues about their Enneagram type.

Remember to observe these patterns over time and in various situations, as people may behave differently depending on circumstances. The Enneagram is a tool for self-awareness and growth, not for labeling or judging others. Use it to assist others in their personal development journey.

OBSERVING EMOTIONAL RESPONSES AND TRIGGERS

When it comes to understanding yourself and others on the Enneagram, it's crucial to pay attention to emotional patterns and triggers. By recognizing these patterns, you can gain insight into how different Enneagram types respond to certain situations. Identifying triggering situations can also help you better understand why certain behaviors or reactions occur, leading to a more accurate typing process.

Recognizing Emotional Patterns

Recognize emotional patterns on the Enneagram by observing emotional responses and triggers. This is crucial for effective service to others. Consider these three key aspects:

- Observe how emotions reveal themselves in each Enneagram type, like excessive nurturing in Type 2s when triggered, or intense emotional withdrawal in Type 4s.
- Identify triggers that cause emotional reactions. Each type has unique triggers that initiate their specific emotional patterns. For example, a violation of privacy might cause a Type 5 to withdraw emotionally.
- Notice patterns in the strength and length of emotional responses. Some types may have more intense and prolonged emotions, while others may fluctuate more.

Identifying Triggering Situations

Observing emotional triggers helps to understand and identify one's Enneagram type and those of others. Recognizing these triggers is key to aiding others' growth. Be aware of individual emotional responses to events, and what causes feelings of threat, anxiety, or upset - it could be criticism, failure, or feeling ignored.

These triggers offer insights into a person's Enneagram type. For instance, a Type One individual may show anxiety when criticized, as they seek perfection and fear being seen as flawed. Understanding these triggers helps customize your support approach, promoting growth and self-awareness. Remember, assisting others begins with understanding their emotional triggers.

ASSESSING CORE DESIRES AND NEEDS

Understanding core desires and needs is crucial for accurately typing oneself and others on the Enneagram, a tool for personal growth. This understanding reveals motivations behind behaviors, promoting empathy and compassion. Here are three Enneagram types:

1. **Type 1 - The Perfectionist**

- Desire: To be good and do right.
- Need: For integrity, order, and perfection.
- Behavior: Strives for perfection, maintaining high standards.

1. **Type 4 - The Individualist**

- Desire: To be unique and authentic.
- Need: For meaning and significance.
- Behavior: Expresses creativity and seeks deep emotional connections.

1. **Type 7 - The Enthusiast**

- Desire: To experience joy and avoid pain.
- Need: For freedom, variety, and adventure.
- Behavior: Seeks new experiences, avoids boredom, and pursues pleasure.

Knowing these core desires and needs provides insights into our motivations and those of others, enabling empathetic approaches to conflicts, fostering stronger relationships, and creating a compassionate environment.

UNCOVERING CHILDHOOD INFLUENCES AND EXPERIENCES

As you explore the subtopic of 'Uncovering Childhood Influences and Experiences' on the Enneagram, it's important to consider three key points. Firstly, early life shaping plays a significant role in shaping our personality. Secondly, impactful childhood events can leave lasting imprints that influence our behaviors and motivations. Lastly, family dynamics, such as birth order or parental relationships, can greatly impact our development and personality formation. Understanding these points can help you gain insights into the roots of your Enneagram type.

Early Life Shaping

Early life experiences greatly affect Enneagram personality development, with childhood playing a crucial role in forming core motivations, fears, and defenses. There are three main ways early life shapes your Enneagram type:

- Parenting styles can form core beliefs and behaviors. Overprotective or neglectful parenting can lead to feelings of insecurity or abandonment. Parents' expectations, such as success, obedience, or independence, also shape personality development.
- Childhood traumas, like abuse or loss, can deeply influence your Enneagram type by creating ingrained fears and defenses.
- Sibling relationships also impact your Enneagram type. Being the oldest, youngest, or middle child influences your identity, competition, and attention-seeking behaviors.

Understanding these early life factors is vital for accurate Enneagram typing and uncovering childhood influences. This insight can foster personal growth and self-awareness.

Impactful Childhood Events

Examining Enneagram childhood influences, it's vital to grasp the significance of impactful events that shape our identities and influence our Enneagram type. Childhood experiences like trauma, loss, or neglect can leave profound imprints on our personalities, affecting our interactions. For those seeking to serve others, acknowledging and exploring these events is essential. Understanding our past aids us in comprehending our motivations, fears, and behavior patterns. This self-awareness promotes empathy and compassion, enhancing our relationships. Through the Enneagram, we can identify and heal past wounds, improving our effectiveness in serving others.

Family Dynamics Influence

Explore the way family dynamics shape your Enneagram type by examining childhood influences. Family significantly molds our personality and behaviors. Family dynamics influence your Enneagram type through three main ways:

- Parental Role Models: Parents, as role models, heavily influence your development through their behaviors and attitudes. Their traits can be adopted, or coping mechanisms can be developed based on their actions.
- Sibling Relationships: Interactions with siblings can shape your Enneagram type. Factors like sibling rivalry, birth order, and overall family dynamics contribute to defining your personality traits.
- Family Values and Beliefs: Your family's values and beliefs can affect your Enneagram type, molding your worldview, ethical compass, and decision-making.

Recognizing the influence of family dynamics on your Enneagram type offers valuable insights into your personality and behaviors, promoting personal growth and self-awareness.

CONSIDERING STRESS AND GROWTH PATTERNS

Identifying someone's Enneagram type accurately requires an understanding of the stress and growth patterns linked to each type. Noting how people react to stress often reveals behaviors atypical of their usual selves, which can be telling of their Enneagram type. For instance, a perfectionist Type One may turn critical and rigid under stress, while a Type Seven, known for enthusiasm, may become impulsive. Recognizing these patterns can offer insights into their core motivations and fears.

Similarly, growth patterns can highlight an individual's Enneagram type. Each type follows a unique growth path towards a healthier self. For example, a withdrawn Type Five may evolve into a more assertive Type Eight. By observing their personal growth towards self-awareness and emotional health, we can better comprehend their motivations and desires.

In essence, considering stress and growth patterns is crucial for accurately determining individuals' Enneagram types, offering valuable insights for personal development.

UTILIZING ENNEAGRAM ASSESSMENTS AND TESTS

Regular use of Enneagram assessments and tests is an effective method to understand your Enneagram type and that of others. These tools provide insights into personality traits, motivations, and behaviors, fostering self-understanding and awareness of others.

Benefits of using Enneagram assessments include:

1. **Self-awareness:** These assessments reveal your core fears, desires, and defense mechanisms, promoting self-awareness. Understanding your Enneagram type can help identify behavioral patterns causing stress, enabling conscious decision-making and personal growth.
2. **Improved relationships:** Identifying the Enneagram types of others enhances understanding of their motivations and communication styles, fostering empathy and effective communication, thus strengthening relationships.
3. **Personal development:** Enneagram tests are powerful personal development tools. They highlight areas for self-improvement, helping to identify strengths and weaknesses, set meaningful goals, and develop growth strategies. Regular use of these tools can track progress and foster alignment with your authentic self.

Incorporating Enneagram assessments into your self-discovery journey can be transformative, enhancing self-awareness, improving relationships, and enabling personal development, leading to positive change in the world.

SEEKING GUIDANCE FROM ENNEAGRAM EXPERTS

If you want to ensure accuracy when typing yourself or others on the Enneagram, seeking guidance from Enneagram experts is crucial. These experts provide validation and insight that can help confirm your type or identify common mistypes. By consulting with professionals who have deep knowledge and experience with the Enneagram, you can gain a clearer understanding of the system and avoid potential errors in typing.

Expert Validation for Accuracy

Obtain expert validation for precise Enneagram typing through Enneagram specialists. These professionals have devoted years to mastering the Enneagram system, offering insightful guidance. There are three primary reasons to consult with these experts:

- **In-depth knowledge**: These experts possess an extensive understanding of the Enneagram system, its nine types, and their distinguishing nuances. They can identify patterns, behaviors, and motivations not immediately apparent to others.
- **Objective perspective**: These experts provide a neutral perspective during the typing process. They offer unbiased evaluations, allowing for a clearer and more accurate self-perception. Their professional expertise prevents personal biases from interfering with the typing process.

- **Refined assessment tools**: These experts often use sophisticated assessment tools and methodologies for accurate typing. These tools, supported by comprehensive research and experience, offer systematic ways to understand and identify Enneagram types.

Through expert guidance, you can improve your Enneagram typing accuracy, leading to a deeper understanding of yourself and others.

Overcoming Common Mistypes

Seek guidance from Enneagram experts to overcome common mistypes. They have extensive knowledge of the Enneagram system and can assist you in accurately identifying different personality types, including your own. Their insights, clarifications, and challenging questions can help you avoid mistyping and gain a deeper understanding of yourself and others. Their support and guidance are invaluable in your journey of self-discovery and personal growth, so don't hesitate to reach out.

EXAMINING SUBTYPE VARIATIONS WITHIN TYPES

Understanding the three subtype variations within each Enneagram type can enhance knowledge of individual personality patterns. These variations are:

1. Self-Preservation: Focused on basic needs and security, these individuals are diligent and

responsible. They may serve others by providing stability and a safe environment.

2. Social: This subtype values relationships and belonging. They are friendly and seek validation through connections, often serving others by building community and providing emotional support.

3. One-on-One: This subtype focuses on personal achievements and forming close bonds. They are driven and competitive and may serve others by helping them achieve goals and offering guidance.

Understanding these subtype variations allows a more comprehensive grasp of personality patterns, enabling more effective assistance to others, meeting their unique needs and promoting personal growth.

VALIDATING YOUR ENNEAGRAM TYPE THROUGH FEEDBACK

Validating your Enneagram type through feedback from others can enhance your self-understanding and personal growth. By inviting trusted individuals such as close friends, family, or colleagues who understand your personality traits to share their observations, you can gain insights into your behavior patterns. It's crucial to listen without judgment or defensiveness to their feedback, which can reveal unrecognized aspects of your personality.

Seeking feedback from multiple sources can offer a comprehensive view of your Enneagram type as different individuals may provide unique insights based on their experiences with you. However, feedback is not a definitive proof of your type but a useful tool for self-discovery and growth. Use it as a starting point for reflection and exploration of your behaviors' motivations and patterns.

EMBRACING PERSONAL GROWTH OPPORTUNITIES

To leverage the Enneagram for personal growth, consider these three strategies:

- **Self-reflection**: Enhance your self-awareness by examining your thoughts, feelings, and behaviors. Ask yourself why you react a certain way or if there are patterns in your behavior, helping you identify areas for improvement.
- **Seek feedback**: Ask others for feedback to gain insights into your strengths and areas needing growth. Be receptive to constructive criticism as it fosters learning and development.
- **Practice self-compassion**: Be patient and kind to yourself during your growth journey. Acknowledge that growth takes time and mistakes may happen. It's fine to have setbacks as long as you continue to progress.

FREQUENTLY ASKED QUESTIONS

How Can I Use the Enneagram System to Improve My Relationships With Others?

Want to boost your relationships using the enneagram system? It's simple! First, try to get the hang of their drives and fears. When you figure out their Enneagram type, you'll start to understand how they act and talk. The more you know, the more empathy and understanding you can show, creating stronger bonds. Plus, knowing your own type can help you grow as a person. But don't forget, the enneagram isn't for labeling, it's for understanding. Use it right, and you'll see your relationships flourish!

What Are Some Common Misconceptions About the Enneagram System?

Let's clear up some common misconceptions about the Enneagram system. It's not just another personality test, it's a powerful tool for self-discovery and personal growth. Think your Enneagram type is set in stone? Think again! We all have the potential to grow and change. But remember, the Enneagram isn't a magic solution for all relationship issues. It simply helps us understand ourselves and others better. So, why not give it a try? You might be surprised at what you learn.

Can My Enneagram Type Change Over Time?

Absolutely, your Enneagram type can shift as you change and grow. Your personality might evolve due to different life experiences or personal growth, causing your Enneagram type to change too. Remember, the Enneagram isn't a rigid label, it's a tool for self-awareness and understanding. So, don't be afraid to embrace the journey of self-discovery and be ready to welcome changes. Keep going!

Is It Possible to Have Traits From Multiple Enneagram Types?

Absolutely, you can exhibit traits from several Enneagram types. Each one of us is unique and often, we show behaviors from more than just one type. Don't think of the Enneagram as a box you have to fit into, instead, use it as a guide for self-understanding and growth. Celebrate your uniqueness and dive into exploring different aspects of your personality. By recognizing and accepting these traits, you're better equipped to steer your personal journey and manage your relationships.

How Can I Apply the Enneagram System to My Professional Life?

You know what? Using the Enneagram system in your work life can totally change the game for you. Think of it as a secret tool that lets you really get who you and your coworkers are. By figuring out your Enneagram type and the types of your coworkers, you'll see what drives you all, your strengths, and even the things you might not see about yourselves. This means you can talk to each other better, build tight-knit relationships, and handle any conflicts with style. The best part? It helps you do your best in your job and make your workplace a great place to be.

CONCLUSION

Ready to dive into the fascinating world of the Enneagram? Getting a handle on your Enneagram type – and those of the people around you – is all about looking inward. You'll need to reflect on yourself, understand your motivations and fears, and recognize your behavioral patterns. It's not always easy, but don't worry, expert guidance is always available!

And here's a fun fact to get you started: According to The Enneagram Institute, the most popular Enneagram type is Type Nine, which makes up 14-20% of the population. Isn't that interesting? Learning about the Enneagram system isn't just a fun exercise – it's a journey of self-discovery and personal growth. So, are you ready to embark on this journey with us in this new chapter?

CHAPTER 13
USING THE ENNEAGRAM FOR PERSONAL GROWTH AND DEVELOPMENT

Are you set to reveal your true potential and embark on a self-discovery journey? Let's dive into the fascinating world of the Enneagram. In this chapter, you'll discover unique personality types that paint a picture of who you are. From the meticulous Perfectionist to the harmonious Peacemaker, each type provides valuable insight and a chance for personal growth. By knowing and applying your Enneagram type's wisdom, you'll gain a deeper understanding of yourself and others - a stepping stone to personal development and a more enriching life. Exciting, isn't it?

UNDERSTANDING ENNEAGRAM TYPES

To leverage the Enneagram for personal growth, a deep comprehension of the various types is crucial. This understanding will offer insights for self-discovery and effective service to others.

The Enneagram system includes nine unique personality types with distinct thought, emotion, and behavior patterns. Getting familiar with these types can boost empathy and compassion.

A thorough understanding of these types offers a framework to comprehend your motivations and behaviors and those of others, enhancing relational navigation and promoting compassionate service.

TYPE 1: THE PERFECTIONIST

As a Type 1, embracing imperfections can be challenging, but it is vital for your personal growth and development. It's important to remember that perfection is subjective and striving for it can lead to unnecessary stress and self-criticism. Instead, focus on finding a balance between setting high standards and being kind to yourself when things don't go exactly as planned.

Embracing Imperfections for Growth

To grow by embracing imperfections, as a Type 1: The Perfectionist, you must acknowledge your flaws. Your desire to serve others might make you strive for perfection, but realizing no one is perfect can fuel personal development. Here's how to accept your imperfections:

- Show self-compassion: Be kind and understanding with yourself when you err or don't meet expectations.

- Release control: Understand plans may change and learn to be spontaneous and flexible.
- Prioritize progress over perfection: Focus on your improvements and the lessons you gain, rather than flawlessness.
- Seek support: Find a supportive community or mentor for guidance and encouragement in your journey of imperfection acceptance.

Balancing High Standards

Balance your high standards as a Type 1: The Perfectionist by setting achievable expectations. Recognize that perfection isn't always possible and aim for progress and improvement instead. Understand that mistakes are part of learning and growth. Allow yourself to make errors, viewing them as growth opportunities rather than failures. Remember that perfection is about accepting imperfections and continuously striving to better yourself. By setting attainable goals and practicing self-compassion when you don't meet them, you can uphold your high standards while promoting self-growth. Remember, to effectively serve others, you must first serve yourself.

Overcoming Self-Criticism Mindset

To overcome self-criticism as a Type 1: The Perfectionist, prioritize self-compassion and accept personal growth's imperfections. Understand that being human involves making mistakes. Here are strategies to defeat self-criticism and foster a compassionate mindset:

- Embrace self-acceptance: You're enough with all your flaws.
- Counter negative self-talk: Swap self-critical thoughts with positive affirmations.
- Applaud progress over perfection: Celebrate small steps towards your goals.
- Seek supportive surroundings: Find a supportive community or mentor for encouragement and perspective.

TYPE 2: THE HELPER

As a Type 2, you are known for your selflessness and willingness to help others. However, it is important to establish boundaries and take care of your own needs as well. Understanding your motivations, such as the desire to be needed and loved, can help you find a healthier balance between giving and receiving in your relationships.

Helper's Selflessness and Boundaries

For Helpers (Type 2) to remain selfless and avoid burnout, it's crucial to establish clear boundaries. To do this, learn to say 'no' without guilt, prioritize self-care, delegate when overwhelmed, and communicate your limits assertively. These steps ensure you have the necessary energy and emotional capacity to continue serving others. Remember, self-care enables you to be an effective helper.

Understanding Type 2's Motivations

Understanding the motivations of Type 2, the Helper, is crucial for personal growth. As a helper, you have a strong need to be loved and appreciated, which you seek by serving others. Your self-worth and identity come from being needed, often leading you to prioritize others over yourself. However, this can lead to difficulties in setting healthy boundaries and neglecting self-care. Recognizing these motivations can help balance your service to others with your own well-being.

Balancing Giving and Receiving

To grow personally, it's crucial to strike a balance between giving and receiving. As an Enneagram Type 2 Helper, you naturally prioritize others' needs over yours. Although commendable, you shouldn't neglect self-care. Here are four ways to balance giving and receiving:

- Show yourself compassion: Be as kind and understanding to yourself as you are to others.
- Establish boundaries: Learn to say 'no' and prioritize your well-being.
- Be open to receive help: Accept support when offered.
- Reflect on yourself: Ensure your generosity stems from love, not the need for validation.

TYPE 3: THE ACHIEVER

As an Achiever in the Enneagram Type 3, your main motivation is seeking admiration and recognition for your achievements. You aim for excellence in every aspect of your life due to a deep-seated drive to be viewed as competent and valuable. Your ambitious nature and focus lead to remarkable successes, but remember that true fulfillment is internal, not just from external praise.

Your natural ability to inspire and motivate others is a key asset, but it's essential to balance this with genuine empathy. Serving others should be driven by sincere care, rather than merely seeking validation. For personal growth, be aware of your tendency to seek external approval. Reflect on your motivations to ensure they align with your true self, and learn to value your worth beyond your accomplishments. Balancing your success drive with your service to others will help you thrive as an Enneagram Type 3 Achiever.

TYPE 4: THE INDIVIDUALIST

As a Type 4, you possess a deep emotional depth that fuels your creative expression and self-discovery. However, you may often struggle with feelings of inadequacy and a sense of longing for something more. Understanding and embracing your unique individuality can help you overcome these challenges and fully embrace your authentic self.

Type 4's Emotional Depth

Type 4 individuals, or The Individualists, possess profound emotional depth that contributes to personal growth through the Enneagram. This emotional capacity lets you deeply connect with others, offering support and understanding. Here's how your emotional depth serves others:

- Empathy: You can comfort and validate others due to your empathetic nature.
- Creativity: Your emotional depth inspires creative solutions and innovative thinking.
- Intuition: Enhanced emotional awareness increases your intuition, helping you understand others' needs.
- Authenticity: You create a safe space for vulnerability by staying true to yourself.

Embracing your emotional depth can significantly impact those around you, fostering their personal growth.

Creative Expression and Self-Discovery

Creative expression and self-discovery are crucial for personal growth in Type 4 Enneagram individuals, who are known for their deep emotional depth and desire for authenticity. Through creative outlets such as art, writing, or music, Type 4s can express their emotions and experiences, exploring their inner self and connecting deeply with others. Self-discovery involves introspection of motivations, fears, and desires, leading to a better self-understanding. By embracing creativity and self-discovery, Type 4s can foster personal development and inspire others through their unique perspective and expression.

Overcoming Feelings of Inadequacy

To combat feelings of inadequacy as a Type 4 Ennea-gram, engage in frequent self-reflection and counteract negative thoughts. Acknowledge your uniqueness and valuable input. Embrace your emotions as a creative inspiration source. Surround yourself with supportive people who value your distinctiveness. Find activities that allow self-expression and fulfillment. Show self-compassion, recognizing everyone has insecurities. Focus on your strengths and celebrate your successes, no matter how small. Remember, you are deserving of love, acceptance, and success.

TYPE 5: THE INVESTIGATOR

Type 5 personalities can utilize their investigative nature for personal growth by embracing their curiosity, seeking learning opportunities, and using their analytical skills for self-discovery. Feeding your intellect through books, workshops, or online courses can foster personal development.

Further, use your investigative skills to understand yourself better by reflecting on your thoughts, feelings, and actions. Journaling can assist in this process, helping to highlight strengths, weaknesses, and areas to work on.

Practicing active listening can also be beneficial, as asking insightful questions and listening attentively to others can lead to empathy, compassion, and a broader perspective.

However, it's important to balance your investigative nature with self-care. Avoid excessive solitude and overthinking, which can inhibit growth. Seek to engage with others, join group activities, and share your knowledge.

TYPE 6: THE LOYALIST

As a Type 6 personality, your loyalty can fuel personal growth. Utilize your supportive nature for self-improvement by:

- **Creating a supportive network**: Surround yourself with inspiring individuals who resonate with your values, aiding your personal growth.
- **Confronting your fears**: Overcome your tendency to worry by facing fears directly, building resilience and strength.
- **Seeking guidance**: Reach out to trusted mentors for advice. Their experience can help navigate tough situations.
- **Practicing self-compassion**: Understand that personal growth is a journey with potential mistakes. Treat yourself with kindness, mirroring the loyalty you show others.

Harness your loyalty for self-improvement and service to others. Embrace strengths, confront fears, seek help, and practice self-compassion to unlock your potential and lead a fulfilled, purposeful life.

TYPE 7: THE ENTHUSIAST

As a Type 7 personality, the Enthusiast, you possess an infectious zest for life which can be harnessed for personal growth. Balancing your adventurous spirit with stability and commitment can enhance your relationships and pursuits. Cultivating mindfulness can help you appreciate the present, despite your tendency to chase the next exciting thing. Techniques like meditation or journaling can facilitate this. Your natural enthusiasm and positivity can uplift others, inspiring them to follow their passions. As an Enthusiast, by balancing exploration and commitment, being mindful, and using your energy to inspire others, you can further personal growth and positively affect others.

TYPE 8: THE CHALLENGER

As a Type 8 Challenger, harness your assertiveness, embrace your innate leadership abilities, and motivate others. Utilize these strategies for personal growth:

- **Lead with integrity**: Guide others honestly and inspire trust through your sense of justice.
- **Empower others**: Identify potential in others and support them in fulfilling it. Encourage their ideas and assist when required.
- **Listen actively**: Even though your assertiveness makes you a natural leader, remember to actively listen and genuinely consider others' viewpoints to foster collaboration.

- **Manage conflicts constructively**: As a Challenger, confrontations may be commonplace. Handle conflicts respectfully, seeking win-win resolutions instead of dominating.

TYPE 9: THE PEACEMAKER

As a Type 9 Peacemaker, you naturally create harmony and balance, skillfully avoiding conflict and fostering unity. Your main focus is preserving peace, both internally and externally. You excel at understanding varied viewpoints and bridging differences, thanks to your empathy and ability to see the world through others' eyes.

However, you may often neglect voicing your needs and desires. It's essential to realize your opinions are valuable and to strike a balance between accommodating others and asserting yourself.

Beware of your tendency to avoid conflicts and suppress emotions in your quest for harmony. Don't overlook your feelings and needs. Reflect on your desires and set necessary boundaries.

With your innate empathy and peaceful demeanor, you unite people and create tranquil environments. By remaining true to yourself and finding your voice, you can continue serving others without compromising your personal growth and development.

APPLYING ENNEAGRAM FOR PERSONAL GROWTH

To use the Enneagram for personal growth, first identify your core type, then delve into its patterns and motivations. Here are four effective ways to leverage the Enneagram for self-improvement and assisting others:

- **Self-awareness**: Use the Enneagram to reflect on your thoughts, feelings, and actions. Notice patterns and their connection to your core type. This awareness helps identify strengths and weaknesses, enhancing your ability to handle relationships and situations.
- **Emotional intelligence**: The Enneagram aids in developing emotional intelligence by revealing the motivations behind your emotions. Recognizing your usual responses enables healthier and more constructive emotional management, improving your empathy and interpersonal connections.
- **Personal development**: The Enneagram provides a guide for personal growth by pinpointing improvement areas. Knowing your core type lets you address its specific challenges, allowing you to break from limiting patterns and foster healthier behaviors and attitudes.
- **Building relationships**: Understanding the Enneagram can improve your relationships. Recognizing others' core types helps you understand their motivations and desires,

fostering empathy, better communication, and deeper connections.

Applying the Enneagram for personal growth is continuous, necessitating self-reflection and self-compassion, and a readiness for change. This tool can help you better serve others and stimulate personal development in all life aspects.

FREQUENTLY ASKED QUESTIONS

How Can I Determine My Enneagram Type?

Want to know your Enneagram type? Start by doing a bit of soul-searching. Think about what gets you out of bed in the morning, what scares you, and what you dream about. Notice how you react in different situations and how you connect with people. You could also take an Enneagram test or read up on the nine types. You might just find one that feels like a perfect fit. Remember, self-reflection and observation are your best tools for finding your Enneagram type. You got this!

Can I Have Traits From Multiple Enneagram Types?

Absolutely! You can definitely show traits from more than one Enneagram type. Everyone has a main type, but we often see bits of other types popping up, especially when we're under pressure or growing. This is what we call 'wings' in the Enneagram world. Remember, the Enneagram is your personal guide to self-discovery and growth. Embrace and understand all parts of your personality. This will help you improve and become the best version of yourself. Isn't that exciting?

Is It Possible for My Enneagram Type to Change Over Time?

Absolutely, your enneagram type can change as you grow and evolve. This doesn't mean you'll turn into a different type altogether. Rather, you'll likely balance out and pick up traits from other types. Think of the enneagram as your personal growth tool, helping you understand and navigate the many facets of your personality.

How Does Knowing My Enneagram Type Help Me in Personal Growth and Development?

Understanding your Enneagram type can really boost your personal growth. It's like having a personal guidebook that explains why you act the way you do. It helps you spot patterns that might be tripping you up or causing unnecessary worry. This knowledge can help you grow in self-awareness, compassion, and empathy - for yourself and for others. It's a tool that can empower you to transform personally and improve your interactions with those around you. So, dive in and explore your Enneagram type - it could be a game changer!

Are There Any Limitations or Criticisms of Using the Enneagram for Personal Growth?

So, you're wondering if there are any drawbacks or criticisms to using the Enneagram for personal growth? Just like anything else, it's not flawless. Some folks believe the Enneagram might oversimplify our intricate personalities and could encourage self-labeling. Remember, the Enneagram is just one way to understand yourself and it might not click with everyone. Still, a lot of people find it super helpful for boosting self-awareness and fostering personal growth. In the end, it's your call whether it's a handy tool for your journey. Keep going, you're doing great!

CONCLUSION

Ready to unlock your potential and transform your life? The Enneagram is your secret weapon. It's a tool that helps us understand ourselves better. We can spot our strengths, pinpoint our weaknesses, and figure out what motivates us. This isn't just about self-awareness, it's about growing empathy and compassion for ourselves and others. Think of the Enneagram as your personal compass, guiding you through the complex journey of life. It's time to explore your inner landscape and kick-start your personal growth. Let's dive into this exciting chapter.

CHAPTER 14

USING THE ENNEAGRAM IN YOUR RELATIONSHIPS

Looking to boost your relationships a notch higher? Let's dive into how the Enneagram could be your game-changer! By getting a grip on the Enneagram basics and figuring out your type, you'll see how you connect with people in a whole new light. This chapter unpacks the Enneagram's influence on relationships, with handy tips on communication, empathy-building, and tackling obstacles. Be it with your family, pals, or at work, the Enneagram can empower you to build robust bonds and make a meaningful impact on others.

UNDERSTANDING THE ENNEAGRAM BASICS

The Enneagram, a tool for understanding individual personalities, has nine types, each with unique patterns of thinking, feeling, and behavior. Type One, 'The Perfectionist,' strives for righteousness and perfection. Type Two, 'The Helper,' is nurturing and finds self-worth in assisting others. Type Three, 'The Achiever,' is goal-oriented and excels in their chosen fields.

'The Individualist,' Type Four, is deeply emotional and highly values authenticity. Type Five, 'The Investigator,' is introverted and seeks intellectual understanding. Type Six, 'The Loyalist,' is dependable, responsible, and craves security.

'The Enthusiast,' is Type Seven, and is spontaneous and life-loving. Type Eight, 'The Challenger,' is assertive and can be confrontational. Finally, Type Nine, 'The Peacemaker,' is adaptable and avoids conflict for peace.

Understanding these personality types aids in building stronger relationships by fostering empathy and understanding. Familiarizing yourself with the Enneagram basics can be invaluable in understanding others.

IDENTIFYING YOUR ENNEAGRAM TYPE

Understanding your Enneagram type is crucial for gaining insights into your thought patterns and emotions, and enhancing your relationships through self-awareness and empathy. Here are three key steps to finding your Enneagram type:

- Self-reflection: Reflect on your lifelong thoughts, emotions, and behaviors. Question what motivates you and drives your actions. This will deepen your self-understanding and reveal your Enneagram type.

- Exploration: Learn about the nine Enneagram types, their motivations, fears, desires, and behaviors. Keep in mind that your Enneagram type is determined by underlying motivations, not just behavior.
- Seek external feedback: Consult with trusted friends, family, or an Enneagram coach for insights on your personality and behavior. Their perspective can validate or challenge your self-identification, aiding in identifying your Enneagram type.

EXPLORING THE ENNEAGRAM'S IMPACT ON RELATIONSHIPS

Understanding your Enneagram type can give you insight into how it influences your relationships. This powerful tool helps you understand your own and others' behaviors and motivations. Knowing the Enneagram types of those around you can foster deeper sympathy for them.

Every Enneagram type presents unique strengths and challenges in relationships. For instance, Type One, or the Perfectionist, may struggle with high standards for self and others, leading to potential frustration and conflict. Recognizing this can help you cultivate patience and understanding.

Conversely, Type Nine, the Peacemaker, might avoid conflict for the sake of harmony, often neglecting difficult conversations or personal needs. Identifying this pattern can assist you in learning to communicate your needs assertively.

Furthermore, understanding the Enneagram can aid in managing conflicts and disagreements by revealing underlying motivations and fears, enabling empathetic and compassionate responses. This can help find common ground and work towards a mutually satisfying resolution.

COMMUNICATION STRATEGIES FOR EACH ENNEAGRAM TYPE

Now let's talk about how your Enneagram type influences your communication style. Understanding the unique communication strategies for each type can help you tailor your approach in your relationships. By learning how to effectively communicate with others based on their Enneagram type, you can enhance understanding, reduce conflicts, and build stronger connections overall.

Enneagram Type's Communication Styles

Identify your Enneagram type and use its related communication strategies to improve your relationships. Each type has a unique style; Type 1 should be direct and non-judgmental, Type 2 should empathize and assert needs, Type 3 should be goal-oriented and acknowledge others' accomplishments. By adapting your communication style, you can strengthen relationships and positively influence them.

Tailoring Strategies for Types

Adapting communication strategies to each Enneagram type fosters stronger relationships and effective communication. It's crucial to understand each type's unique needs and styles.

For Type 1, communicate directly and concisely, focusing on constructive feedback rather than criticism.

Type 2 appreciates warmth and support; acknowledge their efforts.

With Type 3, focus on goals, provide recognition opportunities, and praise their accomplishments.

For Type 4, offer empathy, validate their feelings, and provide an environment for authentic expression.

Type 5 needs space and privacy, so be patient and allow them time to process.

Provide Type 6 with reassurance and consistent, reliable support.

For Type 7, maintain an upbeat attitude, promoting their creativity and spontaneity.

Type 8 values directness, honesty, and assertiveness; respect their autonomy and avoid power struggles.

Lastly, Type 9 needs a gentle, patient, and understanding approach, encouraging them to express their needs and opinions.

Effective Communication for All

To communicate effectively with each Enneagram type, adapt to their unique communication styles. For Type 1, be direct, clear, and offer constructive feedback rather than criticism. For Type 2, appreciate their efforts, listen actively and allow them to express their needs. For Type 3, be goal-oriented, set clear objectives and let them flaunt their skills. Remember, communication is not one-size-fits-all; tailor it to each Enneagram type for stronger relationships.

BUILDING EMPATHY AND UNDERSTANDING IN RELATIONSHIPS

To build empathy and understanding in your relationships, it is essential to enhance emotional connection and resolve conflicts with empathy. By actively listening and acknowledging the emotions of your partner, you create a safe space for open communication and deeper understanding. Empathy allows you to see things from their perspective, fostering compassion and strengthening your bond.

Enhancing Emotional Connection

Boosting emotional bonds in relationships requires fostering empathy and comprehension. Actively enhancing emotional connection provides a secure environment for loved ones to express vulnerability. Three key methods to build empathy and understanding include:

- **Active Listening:** Give your partner or friend undivided attention without judgment or interruption, demonstrating that their thoughts and emotions are valued.
- **Empathetic Validation:** Recognize and affirm their feelings, even if their viewpoint is not fully understood, assuring them that their emotions are valid and you are there for support.
- **Seeking to Understand:** Ask questions to gain insight into their experiences and perspective, thereby deepening your understanding and strengthening your bond.

Incorporating these practices in your relationships can promote empathy and understanding, resulting in a stronger emotional connection with your loved ones.

Resolving Conflicts With Empathy

To resolve conflicts empathetically, engage in understanding and validating your partner's or friend's emotions. Put yourself in their position, listen to their perspective, and foster open communication. Show genuine interest in their feelings, ask open-ended questions, and acknowledge their emotions without minimizing them. Empathy focuses on understanding and support, not problem-solving. Practice active listening and reflect what you hear for better understanding. This approach can deepen relationships and enhance conflict resolution.

ADDRESSING CONFLICTS USING THE ENNEAGRAM

The Enneagram can effectively resolve relationship conflicts by promoting self-understanding and empathy. By recognizing your Enneagram type, you can better understand your reactions and those of others. The Enneagram aids conflict resolution through:

- **Increased Self-Awareness**: The Enneagram encourages self-reflection, helping you comprehend your behavioral patterns and reactions. This understanding enables you to own your actions and make choices that foster resolution.
- **Improved Communication**: Each Enneagram type has unique communication styles and needs. Understanding these can help you adjust your conflict approach, ensuring effective communication and lessening misunderstandings.
- **Empathy and Understanding**: The Enneagram promotes empathy by revealing the motivations and fears of each type. This knowledge allows you to empathize with others' viewpoints during conflicts, providing a safe space for open discussion and resolution.

Using the Enneagram in your relationships not only strengthens them but also promotes growth and harmony.

NURTURING TRUST AND CONNECTION WITH THE ENNEAGRAM

To nurture trust and connection with the Enneagram, you can focus on building strong emotional bonds and enhancing communication and understanding. By understanding and valuing each other's unique Enneagram types, you can create a safe space for vulnerability and growth in your relationships. This process allows for deeper connections and a stronger foundation of trust to be established.

Building Strong Emotional Bonds

Use the Enneagram to enhance your relationships by fostering trust and connection. This powerful tool provides three key benefits:

- **Self-awareness:** Understanding your Enneagram type enhances insight into your behavior, improving communication with your loved ones.
- **Empathy:** By revealing others' motivations and fears, the Enneagram enables you to empathize more, fostering trust and emotional connection.
- **Conflict resolution:** The Enneagram helps identify conflict dynamics and promotes constructive resolutions, leading to healthier relationships.

Enhancing Communication and Understanding

Use the Enneagram to foster trust and understanding in your relationships. This tool helps you comprehend human interaction complexities by understanding your own and others' Enneagram types. With this insight into communication styles, motivations, and fears, you can empathetically engage in open, honest dialogues. Active listening and validating feelings are crucial. Remember, effective communication involves feedback and adjustments. Guided by the Enneagram, you can build robust connections rooted in trust, respect, and understanding.

USING THE ENNEAGRAM TO NAVIGATE POWER DYNAMICS

Use the Enneagram to understand and manage power dynamics in your relationships. This system offers insights into how power manifests within different personalities, helping foster healthier, balanced relationships. Here are three ways to use the Enneagram:

- **Identify personal patterns**: The Enneagram allows you to recognize your behavior patterns and motives, increasing awareness of your power exertion or response to power imbalances. This knowledge enables conscious decisions, promoting authenticity and vulnerability.
- **Empathize with others**: Different Enneagram types have varying fears, desires, and power relations. Understanding these can cultivate empathy for others' unique power dynamics, leading to sensitive and graceful navigation.

- **Enhance communication**: The Enneagram provides a shared language to discuss power dynamics. Open, honest conversations about power imbalances can yield mutually beneficial solutions. It also offers type-specific communication strategies to cater to individual needs and preferences.

ENHANCING INTIMACY AND EMOTIONAL CONNECTION

Using the Enneagram to explore power dynamics can enhance emotional connections and intimacy by understanding others' unique needs and vulnerabilities. This requires a genuine desire to serve, meeting people where they are. This tool provides insight into individuals' core motivations and fears, fostering empathy and compassion.

To improve emotional connections, actively listen to your partner, focusing on their words, body language, and tone. Validate their emotions and experiences, creating a space for open expression. Tailor your approach to each Enneagram type's emotional needs.

Deepen intimacy by offering support and encouragement. Be a reliable ally to help others feel comfortable expressing vulnerability. Respect their boundaries and patience with their process.

Handle conflicts with understanding and collaboration, not defensiveness. Seek mutually beneficial solutions, respecting compromise.

SUPPORTING PERSONAL GROWTH THROUGH THE ENNEAGRAM

Use the Enneagram to foster personal growth, allowing its insights to highlight areas for development and formulate specific improvement strategies. The Enneagram can enhance self-understanding, providing key insights into motivations, fears, and desires, which can pave the way for self-improvement.

To leverage the Enneagram for personal development, implement these three strategies:

- Practice self-compassion: Understand that personal growth is a process, and mistakes are part of the journey. Treat yourself kindly during challenging times. Acknowledge your strengths and weaknesses without judgment.
- Develop self-awareness: The Enneagram offers a structure to comprehend your behavioral and thought patterns. Reflect on your Enneagram type and its impact on your life. This self-awareness allows you to identify habitual or fear-based actions and choose a different response.
- Establish realistic goals: Determine specific growth areas and create achievable goals. Break these down into daily, manageable steps.

Commend your progress and make necessary strategy adjustments.

RECOGNIZING AND APPRECIATING DIFFERENT PERSPECTIVES

Embracing an open, empathetic mindset enhances your understanding of others' unique perspectives, fostering deeper connections. Acknowledging these varying viewpoints is vital for cultivating strong, harmonious bonds. Everyone's perspective, molded by their unique experiences, beliefs, and values, is valid. Genuine curiosity and active listening in conversations can help appreciate these perspectives. Empathize by envisioning their viewpoint, fostering trust, and openness for sharing thoughts.

OVERCOMING RELATIONSHIP CHALLENGES WITH THE ENNEAGRAM

Are you struggling to understand and connect with your partner? The Enneagram can help you gain a better understanding of each other's personalities, motivations, and fears, allowing you to navigate conflicts more effectively. By using the Enneagram as a tool for resolving conflicts, you can identify the underlying issues, communicate more clearly, and find solutions that strengthen your bond.

Enneagram for Better Understanding

Understanding your partner's Enneagram type can enhance your relationship by providing insight into their motivations, fears, and behaviors. This knowledge allows for deeper empathy, recognition of tension-causing behavior patterns, and appreciation of their unique strengths. Using the Enneagram as a guide fosters a relationship based on understanding, compassion, and growth, leading to a fulfilling partnership where both individuals feel valued.

Resolving Conflicts Using Enneagram

Utilize the Enneagram to resolve relationship conflicts by identifying tension roots and employing effective communication. Comprehending both your and your partner's Enneagram types offers insights into behaviors and reactions during disputes. Each type has unique patterns, motivations, and fears that can cause relationship difficulties. Recognizing these and understanding the motivations can enhance conflict resolution. Empathy and willingness to listen are crucial. Use the Enneagram to encourage understanding and compassion for each other's views. Clear communication, active listening, and compromise can help overcome challenges and deepen your connection. The Enneagram isn't a universal solution, but a useful guide for conflict navigation and healthier relationships.

Strengthening Bonds With Enneagram

Utilizing the Enneagram's insights can bolster relationships by understanding each type's unique patterns, motivations, and fears. Three key Enneagram benefits include improving communication by tailoring to styles and preferences, building trust through recognizing and validating fears, and promoting growth and self-aware-ness. These strategies can nurture healthier, more fulfilling relationships that serve both individual and shared needs.

APPLYING THE ENNEAGRAM TO FAMILY RELATIONSHIPS

The Enneagram serves as a valuable instrument for enhancing understanding and communication in family relationships. Recognizing each family member's Ennea-gram type can provide insight into their motivations, fears, and desires, helping to resolve conflicts and strengthen bonds. It aids in identifying each member's strengths and weaknesses. For instance, empathizing with a perfectionist Type One member's sense of respon-sibility and desire for correctness can make them feel valued. Similarly, patient encouragement can help a conflict-avoidant Type Nine member feel comfortable expressing their needs and views. The Enneagram isn't about categorizing people but understanding individual complexities to foster healthier, meaningful relationships. Using it can help nurture compassion, empathy, and acceptance in your family, creating a loving environment for all to flourish.

STRENGTHENING FRIENDSHIPS USING THE ENNEAGRAM

The Enneagram can be used to strengthen friendships by promoting understanding, enhancing communication, and supporting personal growth. Firstly, understanding your friends' Enneagram types can foster deeper connections by allowing you to empathize with their motivations and struggles. Secondly, recognizing the different communication styles of each Enneagram type can help you tailor your conversations to meet your friends' needs, making interactions more fulfilling. Lastly, the Enneagram can guide you in supporting your friends' personal growth journeys by providing insights into their core fears and desires. Using the Enneagram in your friendships can lead to more meaningful and satisfying relationships.

USING THE ENNEAGRAM FOR PROFESSIONAL RELATIONSHIPS

Utilize the Enneagram to fortify professional relationships by enhancing understanding and communication. This system provides insights into the motivations and behaviors of individuals in the workplace, enabling more effective collaboration. Each Enneagram type has unique strengths and challenges that impact their work environment. For instance, Type Ones excel at detail-oriented tasks like quality control but can be overly critical. Recognizing these tendencies allows for constructive feedback and support. Type Threes are ambitious leaders but may grapple with workaholism and fear of failure; acknowledging their work and promoting balance creates a sustainable environment. The Enneagram also aids in conflict resolution and teamwork improvement. Understanding colleagues' motivations and communication styles can lead to mutually beneficial solutions. For example, Type Fours value authenticity and creativity, while Type Sixes prioritize security and loyalty. Respecting these differences fosters an inclusive, collaborative work environment. In summary, applying Enneagram principles in professional relationships can improve communication, conflict resolution, and productivity.

FREQUENTLY ASKED QUESTIONS

How Can the Enneagram Help Me Understand and Improve My Relationships With My Colleagues at Work?

Looking for a way to understand and improve your work relationships? Try using the Enneagram! It's a tool that identifies different personality types. This means you can get a better idea of how your workmates think, feel, and act. It's like having a roadmap to effective communication and conflict resolution. Plus, it can help you build stronger connections at work. By using the Enneagram, you'll develop empathy and appreciate your colleagues' unique strengths and challenges. It's a great way to create a more positive and harmonious office atmosphere. Give it a try!

Can the Enneagram Be Applied to Non-Romantic Relationships, Such as Friendships or Family Dynamics?

Absolutely, you can use the enneagram for non-romantic relationships like friendships or family dynamics! It's a great tool to understand and improve all kinds of relationships. Learning about the different enneagram types and their motivations can reveal why people act the way they do. This knowledge helps you communicate better, show empathy, and forge stronger bonds. Whether it's your friends or family, the enneagram can really boost your relationships.

Are There Any Potential Drawbacks or Limitations to Using the Enneagram in Relationships?

Using the Enneagram can surely boost your relationships. But remember, it's not perfect. You can understand someone's fears and motivations better, but it doesn't neatly box up everyone's behavior. People are a complex mix, after all. So, think of the Enneagram as one tool in your toolbox to improve relationships. Don't just stick with it. Start with it, and then dive into deeper chats and understanding.

Can the Enneagram Help Me Navigate Power Dynamics in Professional Relationships?

Sure, the Enneagram can absolutely help you handle power dynamics at work. By getting to know your own Enneagram type and those of your colleagues, you start to understand how everyone relates to power and leadership. This insight allows you to communicate better, sort out arguments, and cement stronger professional ties. By appreciating everyone's unique needs and viewpoints, you're on your way to creating a more balanced and efficient workplace. So, it's definitely worth a shot!

Is It Possible to Use the Enneagram to Address Conflicts in Family Relationships?

Can the Enneagram help solve family conflicts? Yes, it can! The Enneagram is like a secret weapon that helps you get to know yourself and your loved ones better. By figuring out everyone's Enneagram type in the family, you can uncover what drives them, what scares them, and how they communicate. This newfound knowledge can help you empathize and understand each other, making it easier to solve conflicts. So, with the Enneagram at your disposal, you can work towards building a family bond that's stronger and more harmonious. Let's do it!

CONCLUSION

Are you ready to take your relationships to the next level? The Enneagram is your secret weapon. It's like a roadmap for all your relationships - romantic, friendly, professional, you name it. Think of the Enneagram as a tool that shows you the different dynamics that make up your relationships. It's like a painter bringing all the colors to life on a canvas. But here, the canvas is your relationships. Using the Enneagram, you can learn more about yourself and others, build stronger connections, and bring more harmony into your life. This chapter is your starting point. Let's dive in!

CHAPTER 15
USING THE ENNEAGRAM AT WORK

Feeling stuck in your job? Not sure how to tap into your full potential? Let's introduce you to the Enneagram, your new best friend at work. This fantastic tool is all about personal growth and understanding yourself better. It's like having a roadmap to navigate work challenges.

By knowing your Enneagram type and using its strengths, you'll notice a boost in your productivity, communication skills, and emotional intelligence. Ready to discover how to use the Enneagram for a balanced work-life, a satisfying career, and a harmonious work culture?

It's time for you to unlock your true potential and be the star at work.

UNDERSTANDING THE ENNEAGRAM TYPES

To grasp the Enneagram types, become acquainted with the nine unique personality patterns. Each represents a different perspective on the world and a way of interacting with others. This understanding can enhance your relationships both personally and professionally.

The Enneagram system classifies individuals into nine types: the Perfectionist, the Helper, the Achiever, the Individualist, the Investigator, the Loyalist, the Enthusiast, the Challenger, and the Peacemaker. Each has unique motivations, fears, and desires that shape their behavior.

For instance, Helpers exhibit a strong need to be needed and fear being unwanted. They often go the extra mile to assist others, attuned to emotional needs. Understanding this type can help you acknowledge their caring nature and provide needed support.

Similarly, Perfectionists aim for excellence, setting high standards for themselves and others. They fear mistakes and value precision. Recognizing these traits can help provide constructive feedback and promote their growth.

Familiarity with the Enneagram types can improve your communication, build stronger relationships, and enable better service to others. The key is empathy, understanding, and support for each type's unique needs and goals.

IDENTIFYING YOUR ENNEAGRAM TYPE

To determine your Enneagram type, consider your unique motivations, fears, and desires. Follow these four steps:

1. Self-Reflection: Introspect to understand your inner drives, desires, and fears. This awareness can help identify your Enneagram type.
2. Observing Patterns: Monitor your thoughts, emotions, and behaviors to identify consistent patterns. These can hint at your Enneagram type.
3. Seeking Feedback: Ask trusted individuals for their perspective on your personality traits. Their insights can help clarify your Enneagram type.
4. Self-Acceptance: View the Enneagram as a self-development tool. All types are equal, each having strengths and areas for improvement. Embrace your unique qualities to serve others in alignment with your Enneagram type.

UTILIZING THE ENNEAGRAM FOR SELF-AWARENESS

Are you looking to grow personally and enhance your self-understanding? Utilizing the Enneagram can be a powerful tool for self-awareness. By understanding your Enneagram type, you can gain valuable insights into your motivations, behaviors, and patterns of thinking. This self-awareness can lead to personal growth, improved relationships, and a deeper understanding of yourself.

Enneagram for Personal Growth

Leveraging the Enneagram for personal growth cultivates self-awareness and boosts workplace effectiveness. Here's how it can foster self-discovery:

1. Understanding motivations: The Enneagram illuminates your core fears, desires, and motivations, enhancing self-awareness and empowering you to make informed choices that improve your interactions.
2. Identifying strengths and weaknesses: The Enneagram pinpoints your unique strengths and weaknesses, helping you to capitalize on your strengths and address areas for growth, thus boosting workplace effectiveness.
3. Building empathy and compassion: By revealing different perspectives and motivations, the Enneagram encourages empathy and compassion, which in turn foster stronger relationships and collaboration.
4. Nurturing personal growth: The Enneagram serves as a guide for self-improvement, directing you to become the best version of yourself in both professional and personal spheres.

With the Enneagram, you can undertake a journey of self-awareness and personal growth, enhancing your workplace effectiveness and ability to serve others.

Enhancing Self-Understanding Using Enneagram

Use the Enneagram to boost self-understanding, vital for effective service to others. This tool provides insight into your personality and motivations, exposing core fears, desires, and behavioral patterns. Identifying your Enneagram type helps you recognize strengths and areas for improvement, enhancing your authenticity and compassion in serving others. It offers a framework for understanding diverse perspectives and behaviors, improving empathy and connection with others. The Enneagram also promotes mindfulness of reactions and triggers, enabling conscious responses over impulsive reactions. Hence, using the Enneagram is a crucial step towards personal growth and improved service to others.

Benefits of Self-Awareness

Regular use of the Enneagram for self-awareness offers numerous advantages. It helps you identify your strengths and areas to improve, enhancing personal growth and work efficiency. The Enneagram uncovers your motivations and behavioral patterns, enabling conscious choices and purposeful actions. It improves communication and relationships by fostering understanding and empathy. Additionally, it raises emotional intelligence, facilitating effective emotion management, decision-making, and composed response to challenges. Thus, the Enneagram can lead to a more satisfying and successful professional life.

LEVERAGING YOUR ENNEAGRAM TYPE FOR PRODUCTIVITY

Boost your work productivity with your Enneagram type. Recognizing your Enneagram type offers insights into your strengths, motivations, and growth areas, which can improve productivity and workplace contributions.

Type Ones, with natural perfectionism and responsibility, should prioritize tasks and structure workflows for productivity. Set concise goals, break them into manageable steps for progress, and organization.

Type Twos can improve productivity by utilizing their interpersonal skills to foster strong relationships with colleagues and clients. Understand their needs, provide support, but maintain healthy boundaries and manage your workload.

Type Threes, driven by success, should set ambitious goals, break down large projects, track progress, and leverage their charisma and adaptability. Remember to take breaks and practice self-care.

Type Fours can enhance productivity by using their creativity and unique perspectives. Incorporate artistic elements into work, strive for authenticity, but avoid perfectionism and self-doubt.

Type Fives should allocate time for focused work, create a distraction-free workspace, and engage in stimulating activities. Balance your need for solitude with collaboration opportunities.

Type Sixes can improve productivity by using their analytical skills to anticipate problems and mitigate risks. Collaborate to build a support network, manage anxiety, and seek reassurance when needed.

Type Sevens should set realistic goals, prioritize tasks, and avoid multitasking. Practice mindfulness to maintain focus and avoid distractions.

Type Eights can boost productivity by using their leadership skills, inspiring others, and delegating tasks. Be mindful of your intensity, practice active listening, and collaborate for a productive work environment.

Type Nines should set clear boundaries, prioritize their needs, communicate effectively, and avoid procrastination. Break tasks into manageable steps and collaborate to foster teamwork.

ENHANCING COMMUNICATION WITH THE ENNEAGRAM

To enhance communication with the Enneagram, it's important to understand how it relates to team dynamics. By recognizing and appreciating the different communication styles of each Enneagram type, you can foster stronger connections and collaboration within your team. Additionally, overcoming communication barriers, such as misinterpretation and misunderstanding, can be achieved by applying the insights gained from the Enneagram framework.

Enneagram and Team Dynamics

Use the Enneagram to improve team communication by understanding each member's personality type. The Enneagram benefits team dynamics in four ways:

1. It boosts self-awareness, aiding team members in effectively conveying their needs and preferences.
2. It aids in understanding others' motivations and behaviors, fostering empathy, minimizing conflict, and promoting transparent communication.
3. It encourages appreciation and cooperation by recognizing each member's unique strengths and perspectives, increasing collaboration and productivity.
4. It provides tools for effective conflict resolution by addressing motivations and communication styles, facilitating respectful and productive dialogue.

Integrating the Enneagram into your team dynamics enhances communication, fosters teamwork, and promotes a harmonious, productive work environment.

Understanding Communication Styles

Leveraging the Enneagram to comprehend various communication styles can enhance team communication.

The Enneagram, which identifies nine distinct personality types and their communication styles, can offer insights into individual preferences. Recognizing these styles can foster a harmonious and productive work environment. Tailoring your communication to match each team member's style can improve collaboration and efficiency, ultimately helping to achieve shared goals.

Overcoming Communication Barriers

Use the Enneagram to overcome communication barriers effectively. First, recognize your personal communication style and adjust it according to diverse personalities. Second, understand the nine different Enneagram personality types to tailor your communication for better understanding. Third, practice active listening, responding respectfully and thoughtfully. Lastly, foster empathy and compassion to understand others' perspectives for open and effective communication. Thus, using the Enneagram can help break communication barriers and produce a harmonious work environment.

OVERCOMING CHALLENGES WITH ENNEAGRAM INSIGHTS

Utilizing Enneagram insights is crucial to address workplace challenges effectively. The Enneagram helps us understand ourselves and others, enabling us to tackle hurdles and promote healthy relationships at work. Insights into the different Enneagram types help us strategize against common professional obstacles.

Workplace conflict, whether with a coworker or superior, can hinder productivity and teamwork. Using Enneagram insights, we can understand others' motivations and fears, enabling empathetic and compassionate conflict resolution. For instance, dealing with a confrontational Type Eight requires a direct and assertive approach, recognizing their need for control.

Workplace stress is another challenge. High stress levels often stem from demanding workloads and performance pressure. By recognizing our Enneagram type and stress responses, we can manage stress effectively. For example, a Type Three, driven by success and recognition, should set boundaries and prioritize self-care to avoid burnout.

In short, the Enneagram is a potent tool for overcoming workplace challenges. By applying Enneagram insights, we can resolve conflicts empathetically, understand stress responses, and foster a harmonious, productive work environment. Embrace the Enneagram's power to maximize your workplace potential.

BUILDING EFFECTIVE TEAMS WITH THE ENNEAGRAM

Utilizing the Enneagram to construct effective teams involves leveraging individual strengths and fostering collaboration. Comprehending each member's unique qualities and motivations allows for an environment where everyone can contribute at their best. Here are four ways the Enneagram can be used:

1. **Appreciate diversity**: The Enneagram shows that each member brings unique perspectives and strengths. Embrace this diversity and use it for the team's benefit. Promote open communication and ensure diverse viewpoints are heard.

2. **Assign roles based on strengths**: The Enneagram reveals individual strengths and weaknesses. Assign roles that match each member's talents, leading to greater fulfillment, motivation, and improved team performance.

3. **Foster collaboration and communication**: Use the Enneagram to enhance communication and collaboration within the team. Encourage open sharing of thoughts and ideas, and create a safe space for constructive feedback to minimize conflicts.

4. **Support and development opportunities**: The Enneagram identifies areas for growth. Provide resources to improve these areas, such as training, mentoring, and coaching. This not only helps individual growth but also strengthens the team.

USING THE ENNEAGRAM TO IMPROVE LEADERSHIP SKILLS

If you want to become a better leader, the Enneagram can be a valuable tool. By understanding your own Enneagram type and the types of those you lead, you can enhance your leadership skills and create a more effective and harmonious work environment. The Enneagram offers insights into different leadership styles and can help you adapt your approach to better connect with and motivate your team.

Enneagram for Leadership

Use the Enneagram framework to boost your leadership skills by gaining insights into your personality and behavior. Knowing your Enneagram type can improve self-awareness, enhance communication, foster emotional intelligence, and aid in conflict resolution. Embracing the Enneagram can help you lead authentically and compassionately, inspiring and empowering your team.

Enhancing Leadership Through Enneagram

The Enneagram framework can enhance your leadership skills. It provides insights into nine personality types which helps understand your own and your team's leadership style. This knowledge enables you to adjust your approach and communication to suit your team's needs, promoting a productive work environment. The Enneagram also identifies areas for personal growth, offering chances to bolster your leadership skills. By recognizing your strengths and weaknesses through self-reflection, you can work towards becoming an effective and empathetic leader, improving outcomes for you and your team.

Enneagram and Effective Leadership

Use the Enneagram framework to enhance your leadership skills by understanding your own and your team's personality types. It aids in four key areas: self-awareness, understanding others, conflict resolution, and motivation. By recognizing your strengths and weaknesses, you can improve as a leader. Understanding your team's motivations and behaviors allows effective communication and a positive work environment. The Enneagram also offers insights into conflict management, facilitating tailored mediation, and resolution. By grasping your team's Enneagram types, you can better motivate and engage them, fostering productivity and satisfaction. Incorporating Enneagram into your leadership style can lead to a more successful work environment.

HARNESSING THE ENNEAGRAM FOR CONFLICT RESOLUTION

Use the Enneagram to navigate and resolve workplace conflicts. The Enneagram allows you to understand your personality type and those of your colleagues, offering insight into the motivations, fears, and behaviors that contribute to conflict. This understanding guides you to manage conflicts with empathy, not judgment.

When conflicts arise, use the Enneagram to understand your reactions and triggers, helping you manage your emotions and respond effectively. The Enneagram also helps you understand others' motivations and perspectives, fostering empathy, collaboration and problem-solving.

In conflict resolution, active listening and validating others' emotions are crucial. The Enneagram helps you recognize how different types express emotions, promoting open communication and collaboration.

ACHIEVING WORK-LIFE BALANCE WITH THE ENNEAGRAM

To maintain a balanced work-life, evaluate your Enneagram type's tendencies and devise strategies to meet your personal needs. This will foster a balanced work and personal life. Here are four ways to achieve this using the Enneagram:

1. Understand your Enneagram type: Gain insights into your Enneagram type to understand how it shapes your behaviors, motivations, and reactions. This self-awareness will help you identify overworking tendencies or life aspects you may be neglecting.
2. Set boundaries: Set clear work-life boundaries by defining work hours and disconnecting from work afterward. This will ensure time for self-care, hobbies, and quality time with loved ones.
3. Prioritize self-care: Make self-care compulsory. Identify rejuvenating activities and include them in your routine. Such activities will revitalize you and help maintain work-life balance.
4. Delegate and ask for help: Understand that you can't do everything alone. Delegate work tasks and seek help when needed. Don't shy from

seeking family, friends, or professional help for personal responsibilities. This will lessen the load and allow focus on both work and personal life.

CULTIVATING EMOTIONAL INTELLIGENCE THROUGH THE ENNEAGRAM

Utilizing the Enneagram is crucial for fostering emotional intelligence, particularly for those who aspire to serve others at work. The Enneagram enables you to comprehend your own emotions and responses better, thereby helping you manage challenging situations more effectively.

Besides self-awareness, it aids in developing empathy and compassion by recognizing various Enneagram types and their emotional patterns. This insight allows you to empathize with your colleagues or clients' perspectives and needs, and tailor your communication accordingly.

Furthermore, the Enneagram promotes emotional regulation skills, which includes managing your own emotions and assisting others in doing the same, contributing to a positive, understanding, and harmonious work environment.

APPLYING THE ENNEAGRAM TO CAREER DEVELOPMENT

Using the Enneagram for career development offers insights into your strengths, motivations, and growth areas, aiding in effective decision-making for your career trajectory. Here's how you can utilize it:

1. Unearth your strengths: The Enneagram reveals your unique talents and motivations, which can be leveraged for career success. It also aids in choosing roles and industries that match your skills.
2. Understand your motivators: Every Enneagram type has unique motivations. Comprehending these helps align your career with your values and passions, fostering job satisfaction and fulfillment.
3. Discover growth areas: The Enneagram illuminates areas for improvement. Acknowledging these can help you seek learning opportunities and overcome challenges that hinder your professional growth.
4. Improve communication and collaboration: Insights from the Enneagram into various personality types can enhance relationships and collaboration, promoting teamwork, productivity, and a positive work environment.

INTEGRATING THE ENNEAGRAM INTO ORGANIZATIONAL CULTURE

Incorporating the Enneagram, a potent personality model, into your organizational culture can boost employee engagement and cultivate a unified, efficient work atmosphere. This can be achieved through workshops and training sessions to educate employees about different Enneagram types, fostering self-awareness and better team dynamics, which result in enhanced communication and conflict resolution.

Inclusion of the Enneagram in performance evaluations and goal-setting allows for personalized goals aligned with each employee's natural skills and inclinations, leading to improved engagement and job satisfaction. Leadership and management can benefit from understanding team members' Enneagram types, enabling them to adapt their style to support and motivate individuals effectively, thereby improving morale and fostering a positive work culture.

FREQUENTLY ASKED QUESTIONS

How Can the Enneagram Be Used to Improve Workplace Relationships and Collaboration?

Looking to boost your workplace relationships and collaboration? The Enneagram is a super useful tool for that! It's all about understanding your co-workers' unique personality types and what makes them tick. With this knowledge, you can communicate and work together more effectively. Plus, the Enneagram encourages empathy and compassion, which helps you see things from your colleagues' point of view. This leads to better understanding and teamwork, making your workplace more harmonious and productive. So, why not give it a shot?

Are There Any Potential Drawbacks or Limitations to Using the Enneagram in a Work Setting?

Remember, using the Enneagram at work has its pros and cons. Think of it as just one tool in your toolbox, not the entire kit. Yes, it can boost self-awareness and understanding, but don't solely depend on it for making decisions or evaluating people. Some folks could find it a bit too rigid in categorizing individuals. So, use it as a springboard, not as a crutch. Keep pushing your boundaries and exploring other opportunities for growth.

What Strategies Can Be Employed to Effectively Integrate the Enneagram Into an Organization's Culture?

Bringing the Enneagram into your company culture? Great idea! Start simple: encourage self-awareness and personal growth. Get your team to explore their Enneagram types and see how these play out at work. Provide training and resources so they can easily apply Enneagram insights to their daily lives. Open up the conversation – let's chat about our types and learn from each other. This way, we can boost communication, work better together, and grow individually. Sounds pretty good, right?

Can the Enneagram Be Used to Address Conflicts or Tensions Within a Team or Department?

Is the enneagram useful in resolving team conflicts? You bet! Imagine the enneagram as a guide, steering you through rough times towards peace. It aids in understanding what drives each team member and what scares them, creating empathy and kindness. With this insight, you can tackle conflicts directly, finding shared ground and developing stronger bonds. The enneagram is an effective tool for crafting a balanced and efficient work atmosphere.

How Can the Enneagram Help Individuals Identify and Develop Their Strengths Within Their Career?

Let's talk about the Enneagram and how it can help you in your career. By knowing your Enneagram type, you can discover your natural skills and talents. This helps you focus on what you're good at and what you enjoy. The Enneagram can also guide you on how to boost these strengths. You could do this through training, finding a mentor, or looking for new opportunities. So, go on, use the Enneagram. It's a great way to unlock your potential and excel in your work!

CONCLUSION

Welcome to this exciting chapter on using the Enneagram at work! You've just discovered a powerful key that can unlock your true potential in the workplace. Picture this - a work environment that's not just about tasks and deadlines, but also about self-awareness, productivity, and open communication. It's a place where work-life balance isn't just a buzzword, and emotional intelligence and career development are part of the daily routine.

By incorporating the Enneagram into your company culture, you're paving the way for a more harmonious and satisfying work life. So, gear up to harness the Enneagram's power and prepare to see your personal and professional growth flourish like never before.

CHAPTER 16
USING THE ENNEAGRAM SPIRITUALLY

Searching for a spiritual journey that touches your soul? Your search ends here with the Enneagram. This potent tool guides you on an amazing self-discovery and growth trip. Dive into the nine spiritual paths of the Enneagram and discover yourself and your divine connection at a deeper level. Accept your Enneagram type's shadow side, weave Enneagram practices into your daily life, and foster feelings of compassion and empathy. Hop on for an unparalleled spiritual adventure!

UNDERSTANDING THE ENNEAGRAM'S SPIRITUAL PURPOSE

Understanding the Enneagram's spiritual purpose is vital as it's more than a self-improvement tool; it provides deep insights into one's soul and the divine essence in others, fostering love, compassion, and empathy in relationships. It makes us aware of the unique gifts and challenges of each Enneagram type, enabling us to support others in their spiritual journey, providing safe spaces for self-exploration and spiritual growth.

Moreover, it aids in transcending ego, connecting with the higher self, and highlighting unconscious patterns and motivations behind thoughts, emotions, and behaviors. It helps break free from limiting beliefs, thereby encouraging spiritual growth and service to others.

The Enneagram's spiritual purpose also emphasizes that true happiness comes from giving, not receiving. By embodying your Enneagram type's qualities in a spiritually conscious way, you contribute to humanity's collective awakening.

EXPLORING THE NINE SPIRITUAL PATHS WITHIN THE ENNEAGRAM

As you explore the nine spiritual paths within the Enneagram, you will discover its power as a spiritual guide. It invites you to embrace inner transformation and embark on a journey of self-discovery. Through understanding your Enneagram type, you can uncover your unique divine purpose and cultivate a deeper connection with your spiritual self.

Enneagram as Spiritual Guide

Explore the transformative power of the Enneagram, a spiritual guide offering nine unique paths to self-awareness and spiritual growth. It's more than a personality type system; it's a deep spiritual journey. Delving into it, you'll reveal your soul's depths, discover the patterns and motivations shaping your thoughts, emotions, and behaviors, and gain insight into your core fears and desires. This leads to a better understanding of yourself and others. The Enneagram, a roadmap to spiritual enlightenment, encourages you to embark on a journey of self-discovery, compassion, and service to others.

Embracing Inner Transformation

Embark on a journey of self-transformation through the nine spiritual paths of the Enneagram. Exploring your personality type provides deep insights, guiding you to serve others with more compassion. Embrace this transformation through self-reflection and compassionate action. Reflect on your thoughts, emotions, and behaviors to understand your motivations and identify growth areas. Once you understand your inner workings, use this knowledge to serve others empathetically. This could be through volunteering, lending an ear, or offering help. Remember, this transformation is a lifelong journey that the Enneagram's spiritual paths can help with, leading to self-discovery and service to others.

Finding Divine Purpose Within

Explore the nine spiritual paths of the Enneagram to continue your self-transformation journey and discover your divine purpose. Each Enneagram type provides a unique spiritual blueprint for growth and service. Delving into your type reveals your inherent gifts and talents that can be used for global betterment. The

Enneagram acts as a compass towards your divine purpose, urging you to align your actions with your spiritual essence. By following your type's path, you can develop qualities like compassion, wisdom, and courage, enabling you to authentically serve others with love. The Enneagram's sacred wisdom is the key to uncovering your divine purpose.

USING THE ENNEAGRAM AS A TOOL FOR SELF-REFLECTION IN YOUR SPIRITUAL JOURNEY

Use the Enneagram as a tool for self-reflection and spiritual growth. It's more than a personality system; it's a guide for spiritual transformation. Here's how:

1. **Understanding ego patterns**: It helps identify your ego patterns and motivations, allowing you to see their influence on your thoughts and actions. This awareness lets you detach from your ego and choose actions that align with your higher self.
2. **Discovering your true essence**: The Enneagram uncovers your core divine qualities, hidden by your ego. Self-reflection enables you to identify personality traits aligned or misaligned with your true essence, helping you embody your authentic self and enriching your spiritual journey.
3. **Fostering compassion**: Deepening self-reflection with the Enneagram enhances understanding

and empathy towards yourself and others. This compassion fosters deeper connections and a sense of unity.

4. **Overcoming limitations**: It identifies fears and limitations hindering your spiritual growth. By acknowledging and facing these, you expand your consciousness, step into your highest potential, and lead a more purposeful life.

Incorporate the Enneagram in your spiritual journey for profound insights and transformation. This tool aids in navigating the path towards spiritual growth, benefiting both you and others.

EMBRACING THE SHADOW SIDE OF YOUR ENNEAGRAM TYPE FOR SPIRITUAL GROWTH

Embracing the shadow side of your Enneagram type is essential for your spiritual growth. It is through acknowledging and understanding your shadow that you can catalyze profound transformation. By cultivating self-awareness and delving into the aspects of your personality that you tend to avoid or deny, you can unlock the potential for deep healing and spiritual evolution.

Shadow as Spiritual Catalyst

Utilizing the Enneagram spiritually involves acknowledging and accepting your type's shadow side - the unconscious aspects of your personality - to stimulate spiritual growth. This acceptance can enhance self-awareness and personal growth by deepening your understanding of your patterns and limitations. Additionally, it can foster empathy, enabling you to better understand other's struggles and serve them with compassion. Hence, embracing your shadow side can significantly benefit your spiritual journey and your ability to serve others with love and understanding.

Transforming Through Self-Awareness

Diving into your Enneagram type's shadow side enables a transformative self-awareness journey, fostering spiritual growth. It involves confronting uncomfortable or even shameful personality aspects, exploring your psyche's deeper layers, and acknowledging suppressed or ignored self-parts. Despite its challenge, it's crucial for personal and spiritual growth. By accepting your shadow, you gain a profound self-understanding and insight into your motivations. This also helps cultivate compassion and empathy for others, recognizing our shared human struggles. Through self-awareness, weaknesses become strengths, promoting a sense of wholeness and authenticity.

APPLYING ENNEAGRAM WISDOM TO DEEPEN YOUR CONNECTION WITH THE DIVINE

Use the Enneagram's wisdom to strengthen your Divine connection. This tool provides deep self-understanding, enabling a more profound spiritual journey and enhanced empathy towards others. Here are two ways to use the Enneagram:

1. **Discover Your Divine Essence**: The Enneagram can identify behavioral patterns that block your Divine connection. Through self-awareness and inner work, you can break these patterns and align with your true nature, boosting your Divine connection and opening possibilities for growth.

2. **Transform Your Shadow**: The Enneagram illuminates the unconscious patterns that can hinder your spiritual development. By recognizing and integrating these shadow elements, you can remove barriers separating you from the Divine. The Enneagram offers specific practices for each type, assisting you in overcoming spiritual challenges.

INTEGRATING ENNEAGRAM PRACTICES INTO YOUR DAILY SPIRITUAL ROUTINE

Integrate Enneagram practices into your daily spiritual routine to deepen self-understanding and compassion for others. Use daily reflections to consider your Enneagram type's influence on your thoughts and feelings, promoting mindfulness throughout the day. Engage in Enneagram-inspired affirmations or prayers that align with your type's growth areas and challenges, inviting transformation and healing. Practicing self-observation lets you examine your thoughts and emotions without judgment, aiding in conscious response choices. Incorporate Enneagram-inspired service acts into daily life by understanding other Enneagram types' motivations and needs, providing support on a deeper level. This integration of Enneagram practices can transform your spiritual routine, deepening your connection with yourself, others, and the divine, and fostering a life of increased awareness, compassion, and love.

NURTURING COMPASSION AND EMPATHY THROUGH THE ENNEAGRAM'S SPIRITUAL TEACHINGS

To nurture compassion and empathy using the Enneagram's spiritual teachings, engage in self-reflection and understand others' experiences. Here's how:

- Show self-compassion: Accept your flaws, forgive your mistakes and learn from them.
- Improve active listening: Listen to others without judgment, understand their perspective and recognize their emotions.
- Be curious about others: Ask open-ended questions to understand others deeply.
- Practice perspective-taking: Understand others' experiences and emotions by putting yourself in their place.
- Perform acts of kindness: Serve others and show kindness to foster empathy and compassion.

Incorporating these practices daily can help deepen your connection with others and develop a desire to serve them.

FREQUENTLY ASKED QUESTIONS

How Can I Use the Enneagram to Enhance My Meditation Practice?

Looking to boost your meditation practice? Give the Enneagram a shot! It's a great way to better understand yourself and your habits. By figuring out your Enneagram type, you can tackle specific challenges and seize opportunities to grow during meditation. So, if you're a Type 5, try to focus on being present and ease up on the need for intellectual stimulation. Trust me, the Enneagram is an awesome tool for personal growth and taking your spiritual journey to the next level.

Can the Enneagram Help Me Understand the Spiritual Significance of My Relationships?

Sure, the Enneagram can really help you grasp the spiritual side of your relationships. Let's break it down. You first identify your Enneagram type and the types of those around you. This will shed light on your behavioral patterns and how they affect your relationships at a deeper level. The best part? This newfound self-awareness can help you become more compassionate, empathetic, and understanding in your relationships. In turn, this can fuel your spiritual growth as you tackle the complex world of human interaction. So, why not give it a try? It might be the key to unlocking a new level of understanding in your relationships.

What Are Some Practical Ways to Incorporate Enneagram Practices Into My Daily Prayer Routine?

Want to boost your spiritual journey? Well, let's talk about how you can weave Enneagram practices into your daily prayer routine. First, think about what drives you based on your Enneagram type. Use this insight to shape your prayers. For instance, if you're a Type 2, your prayers could revolve around being thankful for your ability to help others. If you're a Type 5, you might want to ask for wisdom and understanding in your prayers. Syncing your Enneagram knowledge with your spiritual routine can lead to impressive personal growth. So, why wait? Start today and witness the transformation!

How Can I Use the Enneagram to Deepen My Connection With Nature and the Environment?

Looking to feel more in tune with nature and the environment? The Enneagram can really help! Knowing your Enneagram type can shed light on your bond with the natural world and how you can make a positive impact on it. From being mindful in nature, to living sustainably, or standing up for environmental causes, the Enneagram can steer your spiritual journey towards a deeper love for our planet.

Can the Enneagram Be Used as a Tool for Forgiveness and Healing in My Spiritual Journey?

Wondering if the Enneagram can guide you towards forgiveness and healing in your spiritual journey? The answer is a resounding yes! The Enneagram is a fantastic tool that gives you deep insights into your own personality and behaviors. As you understand yourself better, you'll see where you need to forgive and heal. You can then focus on your Enneagram type's growth path to foster compassion and empathy for yourself and others. This way, you'll experience deep forgiveness and healing on your spiritual path. So, why not give it a shot?

CONCLUSION

The Enneagram isn't just a tool, but a powerful ally in discovering your spiritual path and self-reflection. With nine spiritual paths to explore and a shadow side to embrace, you're certain to deepen your connection with the divine.

Making Enneagram practices a daily habit can help you grow in empathy and compassion. And here's a compelling fact - over half of the people who use the Enneagram report feeling more peaceful and experiencing a significant spiritual transformation.

CHAPTER 17

PANELS OF ENNEAGRAM TYPES AND HOW GROUPS OF TYPES INTERACT

Ever wondered how different personalities blend to create a dynamic and strong team? It's just like the varied segments of an enneagram where every type interacts in its unique yet intriguing way. Imagine understanding these interactions and using them to your advantage in personal relationships, work settings, and friendships. By mastering group dynamics, you're on your way to fostering peaceful relationships and making a bigger impact.

UNDERSTANDING ENNEAGRAM PANELS

Grasping Enneagram panels helps understand how different types interact within groups, essential for those wishing to aid others in their personal growth journeys. Each type has unique strengths, motivations, and perspectives, yielding enlightening and challenging interactions. Studying panels provides insights into these interactions, impacting personal development and group relationships.

A crucial aspect to consider is the concept of integration and disintegration. Each type has a specific growth and stress pattern, influencing behaviors and reactions during interactions. Recognizing these patterns can help support individuals in their personal growth by guiding them towards their integration points.

Understanding Enneagram panels also helps identify potential group conflicts and tensions. Since different types perceive and respond to the world differently, misunderstandings or clashes may arise. Awareness of these dynamics can facilitate open communication and understanding among group members.

In essence, understanding Enneagram panels can help support personal growth, navigate conflicts, and foster a harmonious environment. So explore the world of Enneagram panels, and experience the transformative power it has for individuals and groups.

TYPES IN PANEL DYNAMICS

Understanding panel dynamics in the Enneagram involves recognizing the unique qualities and interactions of different types within a group. Consider these four key points:

1. **Type Compatibility:** Certain types naturally align or conflict with others. Recognizing this can

foster a productive panel. For instance, Type 1, known for perfectionism, often aligns with Type 9, who values peace.

2. **Group Roles:** Each type usually adopts specific roles within a panel. Identifying these roles contributes to a balanced, cooperative environment.

3. **Communication Styles:** Each type has a distinct communication style affecting group interactions. Acknowledging these styles can improve understanding and collaboration.

4. **Conflict Resolution:** Understanding each type's approach to conflict can aid in effective resolution, fostering open dialogue.

THE POWER OF GROUP DYNAMICS

Now let's talk about the power of group dynamics. Understanding how group dynamics impact collaboration is crucial for achieving success in any team setting. By harnessing the collective strengths of each individual in the group, you can create a powerful synergy that leads to greater creativity, problem-solving, and overall effectiveness.

Impact of Group Dynamics

Group dynamics' impact is observable in Enneagram-type panels, demonstrating its power in four significant ways:

1. **Empathy boost**: Group membership allows for witnessing others' struggles and victories, enhancing understanding and empathy.
2. **Improved collaboration**: Diverse perspectives and strengths from various Enneagram types lead to better problem-solving and innovation.
3. **Increased self-awareness**: Group dynamics help identify personal patterns and behaviors for potential growth.
4. **Support and accountability**: Groups provide a supportive network for shared goals and accountability.

Embracing group dynamics can foster a nurturing environment that uplifts others while promoting personal growth.

Enhancing Group Collaboration

Group dynamics can boost collaboration by utilizing the strengths and viewpoints of different Enneagram types. Individuals of various Enneagram types contribute distinctive skills and insights, such as Type Ones' meticulousness and responsibility, Type Twos' empathy and support, and Type Fives' intellectual curiosity and analytical thinking. This diversity enables the group to approach complex issues from multiple perspectives and create innovative solutions. The group's collective wisdom helps identify blind spots and challenge assumptions, leading to more comprehensive and effective results. Thus, group dynamics can enhance collaboration by leveraging each Enneagram type's unique strengths.

Harnessing Collective Strengths

To enhance group collaboration, harness the power of group dynamics and collective strengths. This involves four key strategies:

1. **Capitalizing on diversity:** Foster an environment where unique perspectives and skills are valued and everyone feels heard.
2. **Building trust:** Establish a sense of trust and psychological safety, encouraging vulnerability and honest feedback to facilitate collaboration.
3. **Leveraging strengths:** Identify and use each team member's distinct strengths and expertise, assigning tasks that allow them to contribute effectively to the group's success.
4. **Promoting teamwork:** Advocate for collaboration, shared purpose, joint decision-making, and problem-solving to achieve more as a group than as individuals.

INTERACTIONS WITHIN TYPE TRIADS

Understanding type triads' dynamics helps improve relationships. The Gut triad includes Types 8, 9, and 1, where Type 8, the Challenger, and Type 1, the Perfectionist, may clash due to their strong personalities, but can collaborate effectively when respecting each other's boundaries.

Type 9, the Peacemaker, mediates conflicts, bringing harmony.

The Heart triad consists of Types 2, 3, and 4. Type 2, the Helper, seeks validation and support, which Type 3, the Achiever, can provide, resulting in a mutually beneficial relationship. Type 4, the Individualist, adds depth and authenticity.

The Head triad includes Types 5, 6, and 7. Type 5, the Investigator, favors solitude and intellect, while Type 6, the Loyalist, requires security. Type 7, the Enthusiast, adds spontaneity, encouraging Types 5 and 6 to embrace new experiences.

Understanding triad interactions aids in building stronger relationships by leveraging each type's strengths to create a supportive, harmonious environment.

HARMONIOUS INTERACTIONS IN PANELS

Harmonious panel interactions significantly influence the dynamics of Enneagram types. These interactions provide a supportive environment for personal growth and understanding. They have four main benefits:

1. **Mutual Respect**: Harmonious interactions build an atmosphere of respect and acceptance, making each panel member feel valued. This respect encourages open, honest communication and strengthens the panel's dynamics.

2. **Collaborative Problem-Solving**: Harmonious panels enable members to collaboratively solve problems, leveraging their combined strengths and expertise to tackle complex issues effectively. This approach spurs creativity and innovation, resulting in better outcomes.

3. **Empathy and Compassion**: These interactions foster empathy and compassion, with panel members actively listening and understanding each other's experiences and emotions. This empathy creates a supportive environment where individuals can express their vulnerabilities and receive necessary support.

4. **Personal Growth and Development**: Harmonious interactions among Enneagram types facilitate personal growth and development. Panel members can learn from each other's strengths and challenges, gaining new insights and perspectives. This continuous learning enhances individual growth and self-awareness, benefiting the entire panel.

CHALLENGING INTERACTIONS IN PANELS

Now let's explore the challenging interactions that can arise within panels of Enneagram types. Conflict resolution strategies and navigating diverse perspectives will be key points of discussion. It's important to understand how to handle conflicts and differing viewpoints effectively in order to foster healthy and productive interactions within these panels.

Conflict Resolution Strategies

To manage conflicts among Enneagram panels, use these four effective strategies:

1. Practice active listening: Understand others' perspectives by maintaining eye contact, showing empathy, and providing full attention. This can de-escalate conflicts and foster understanding.
2. Encourage open communication: Develop a safe environment for everyone to express their thoughts and feelings openly. This can address underlying problems and stimulate healthy discussions.
3. Seek common ground: Unite the group by focusing on shared goals or values. This can shift attention from differences and encourage cooperation.
4. Collaborate on solutions: Work as a team to devise mutually beneficial solutions, fostering ownership and commitment to the resolution.

Applying these strategies can help create a supportive, inclusive environment where everyone's needs are met, allowing the panel to flourish.

Navigating Diverse Perspectives

When dealing with diverse perspectives in panels, it's vital to maintain open-mindedness and communicate effectively. Always value each viewpoint and use these situations as chances to learn and understand, rather than imposing your beliefs. Show empathy and respect in conversations, acknowledging varying experiences shaping each perspective. Practice active listening to fully grasp others' viewpoints and express your ideas clearly using inclusive language, avoiding jargon. This approach fosters an open-dialogue environment, facilitating collaboration and growth in the panel.

EXPLORING TYPE COMBINATIONS

Examining combinations within Enneagram type panels can yield crucial insights into how various types interact. Key considerations include:

1. **Complementary Pairings**: Specific Enneagram types naturally balance each other. For instance, Type Eight's assertiveness pairs well with Type Nine's calming influence, facilitating the development of effective teams or partnerships.

2. **Conflict Triggers**: Some combinations may cause inherent conflicts. A perfection-driven Type One might clash with rule-disregarding Type Seven. Awareness of such conflicts aids in empathetic conflict resolution.

3. **Growth Opportunities**: Each type combination presents unique growth prospects. Interactions with diverse Enneagram types can stimulate skill and perspective development. Be receptive to learning from others.

4. **Communication Styles**: Understanding different types' communication styles can boost collaboration and prevent misunderstandings. Some types may communicate directly, while others might prefer indirect communication. Adapting your style to others' needs can strengthen connections and support a conducive environment.

Exploring Enneagram type combinations can deepen your understanding of inter-type interactions, empowering you to enhance relationships, promote effective teamwork, and serve others more efficiently.

PANEL DYNAMICS IN PERSONAL RELATIONSHIPS

When it comes to personal relationships, understanding panel dynamics can be crucial. One key aspect to consider is the power dynamics within the relationship. How do you and your partner navigate decision-making and assertiveness? Another important factor is communication patterns and styles. How do you both express your needs and emotions? Finally, conflict resolution strategies play a vital role in maintaining a healthy relationship. How do you and your partner handle disagreements and find resolutions? By exploring these points, you can gain valuable insights into the dynamics of your personal relationships.

Relationship Power Dynamics

In personal relationships, it's vital to comprehend power dynamics among different Enneagram types for healthier interactions. Four key points in relationship power dynamics include:

1. Acknowledging and respecting each other's unique strengths brought by each Enneagram type ensures equality and mutual respect.
2. Promoting open, judgment-free communication is crucial for maintaining a balanced relationship.
3. Shared decision-making fosters equality, giving both parties a valued voice in the process.
4. Flexibility and compromise are essential as power dynamics can change, leading to beneficial solutions for individuals and the relationship.

Communication Patterns and Styles

Exploring communication patterns and styles within Enneagram types in personal relationships can enhance your ability to interact effectively. Each type has a unique communication style that can either strengthen or weaken connections. For instance, Type Ones communicate with a strong moral compass, Type Twos prioritize nurturing, Type Threes are goal-driven and direct, while Type Fours express depth and emotion. Recognizing these patterns allows you to adjust your communication to better cater to others' needs, thus fostering healthier relationships.

Conflict Resolution Strategies

Enneagram-based strategies can efficiently resolve personal relationship conflicts, enhancing relationship health. Consider these four strategies:

1. **Active listening**: Understand the other's viewpoint without interruption. Show empathy and validate their feelings for open communication.
2. **Find common ground**: Seek shared interests or goals for a win-win solution. Focus on agreement areas to foster cooperation and compromise.
3. **Use 'I' statements**: Express your feelings and needs using non-aggressive language to encourage understanding and decrease defensiveness.
4. **Take necessary breaks**: If the conflict intensifies, temporarily step away. Cool down and collect your thoughts before resuming the conversation.

Implementing these strategies can improve your personal relationships. Effective communication and understanding are key to serving others.

PANEL DYNAMICS IN WORK ENVIRONMENTS

Understanding Enneagram panels' dynamics in work environments can improve collaboration and service to others. Each Enneagram type contributes distinct strengths and challenges that influence team dynamics. For instance, the Perfectionist (Type One) might be a meticulous planner, the Helper (Type Two) an empathetic team player, and the Achiever (Type Three) an ambitious driver.

However, each type has unique motivations and fears which impact their behavior. The Challenger (Type Eight) may be assertive but fear vulnerability, while the Peacemaker (Type Nine) may be adaptable but fear conflict.

Promoting open communication and understanding among panel members is essential for a harmonious work environment. Encouraging expression of thoughts and concerns can address conflicts and meet everyone's needs. By acknowledging each Enneagram type's strengths and challenges, a supportive and inclusive workspace can be created.

PANEL DYNAMICS IN FRIENDSHIPS

Understanding friendship dynamics is key to fostering strong relationships among Enneagram types. Friendships, offering emotional support and companionship, are valuable in our lives. Each Enneagram type brings unique strengths and challenges. Consider these four factors for effective friendship dynamics:

1. **Value individual differences:** Each Enneagram type has a unique worldview and life approach. Respect these differences as they enhance the diversity and richness of your friendship.

2. **Engage in active listening:** Solid communication is fundamental in friendships. Actively listen to your friends, regardless of their Enneagram type, to better understand their emotions and experiences, thereby strengthening your bond.

3. **Provide judgment-free support:** Each Enneagram type has specific fears and behaviors. Provide a safe, judgment-free space for your friends to express themselves, while challenging any negative patterns.

4. **Applaud growth and development:** Friendships involve growth and self-discovery. Celebrate your friends' personal development and achievements, offering support and encouragement for their continuous improvement.

NAVIGATING PANEL INTERACTIONS EFFECTIVELY

Successfully navigating panel interactions involves recognizing the distinct dynamics and contributions each Enneagram type brings. This understanding promotes a productive, harmonious environment where all feel valued.

Each Enneagram type has unique strengths and weaknesses, with some being innovative thinkers, others detail-oriented. Valuing these diverse skills enables full potential group realization.

Effective panel interactions also hinge on communication. Be aware of your style and its potential impact. Some types favor assertive communication, others prefer gentleness and diplomacy. Adapting your style to others' needs strengthens connections, minimizes conflicts.

Being receptive to feedback and constructive criticism is also crucial, as each type has growth areas and blind spots. Embracing feedback boosts self-awareness and personal development. The goal isn't perfection, but collective learning and improvement.

Remember, serving others underpins effective panel interactions. Instead of being self-focused, strive to understand and support others' needs. Practicing empathy and compassion fosters an inclusive, respectful environment.

FREQUENTLY ASKED QUESTIONS

How Can Individuals in Different Enneagram Types Best Communicate and Understand Each Other in a Panel?

Want to communicate better with different Enneagram types in a panel? Start by actively and empathetically listening. Don't let differences distract you, focus on making connections instead. Encourage conversation by asking open-ended questions and make sure everyone feels safe to express themselves. Be patient and understanding. Remember, everyone sees things differently. When you celebrate these differences and promote open communication, you're setting up a rich, harmonious panel experience for everyone.

What Are Some Common Challenges That Arise When Working in a Panel With Individuals From Different Enneagram Types?

So, you're working on a team with different Enneagram types, huh? It can be a bit tricky, not gonna lie. Miscommunication and misunderstandings can happen because everyone sees things a bit differently. But don't worry, different approaches to tasks and decision-making can actually be a good thing too! Just remember to be patient, keep an open mind, and appreciate the unique insights everyone brings. By promoting a team spirit based on empathy and collaboration, you'll find that these challenges aren't so tough after all. Keep going, you're doing great!

Are There Any Specific Strategies or Techniques for Managing Conflicts Within a Panel of Enneagram Types?

Looking for ways to handle conflicts in a group with different enneagram types? Let's get right to it. Conflicts are often because of the diverse views and motivations of each type. Here's what can help - promote open communication, actively listen, and boost empathy in your group. Try using conflict resolution techniques like compromise and collaboration to find win-win solutions. Just remember, a group that works well together can collaborate better and serve more effectively. So, let's make that happen!

How Can Panel Dynamics Be Utilized to Enhance Personal Growth and Development?

Here's a simple way to boost your personal growth: get to grips with group dynamics. Understand the good and bad points of everyone in the group and use them to work better together. Listen carefully to what others have to say and be open to different viewpoints. It's a great way to challenge your own ideas. Remember, stepping out of your comfort zone and learning from others is a sure-fire way to grow.

Can Enneagram Panels Be Used as a Tool for Team-Building and Improving Collaboration in a Work Environment?

Absolutely! Enneagram panels are a great way to boost team-building and collaboration at work. They help mix up different enneagram types, which brings diverse viewpoints to the table, sparking fresh and innovative ideas. Plus, they help team members understand and appreciate each other's unique strengths and challenges. So, they can really help your team work together more effectively and cohesively. Give it a try, and watch your team grow stronger!

CONCLUSION

The Enneagram is key to creating smooth relationships both in personal life and at work. Did you know a whopping 85% of people have found their interactions within type triads to be really helpful and life-changing? By simply understanding and valuing the unique traits of each Enneagram type, we can steer way through panel interactions effectively and create strong bonds with others. So, why not harness the power of the Enneagram? It can unlock a wealth of potential for growth and understanding in your relationships.

CHAPTER 18

WARNINGS ABOUT MISUSING THE ENNEAGRAM

Ready to dive headfirst into the captivating realm of the Enneagram? Hold on! There are some serious pitfalls you need to watch out for. Misusing this potent tool can have some pretty serious repercussions. It's like walking a tightrope without any safety net. One wrong move and you might find yourself in the middle of misinterpretations, manipulations, and avoidance. But don't sweat it! This chapter is your guide to navigating these hazards, ensuring you use the Enneagram in a way that uplifts and empowers others.

MISINTERPRETING ENNEAGRAM TYPES

Avoid misinterpreting Enneagram types by acknowledging the complexities beyond surface-level descriptions. The Enneagram, a tool for self-awareness and growth, isn't just about simple categorizations. Each type is multi-faceted, with various behaviors, motivations, and fears. To understand each type's intricacies, it's vital to delve deeper and refrain from making assumptions.

Relying solely on superficial descriptions can lead to oversimplification and overlook each individual's unique nuances. The Enneagram's purpose is not to box people in, but to provide insight into their core motivations and behavior patterns, thereby helping them in their personal growth journey.

To comprehend Enneagram types accurately, it's important to explore the underlying motivations and fears that drive each type, requiring active listening, empathy, and a willingness to go beyond surface descriptions. This way, you can better assist others in their self-discovery and development.

The Enneagram is designed to empower, not confine individuals. Embrace each type's complexities to deepen your understanding of others and contribute to their growth and well-being. Therefore, explore the Enneagram's depths and avoid misinterpretation based on superficial descriptions.

USING ENNEAGRAM AS A LABELING TOOL

Avoid using the Enneagram merely as a labeling tool as this dilutes its actual purpose of fostering self-awareness and personal growth. Here are some reasons to avoid this practice:

- It simplifies complex individuals: Labeling people by their Enneagram type can overlook the richness of their personality and lead to stereotyping, hindering understanding.
- It fosters fixed mindsets: Labeling reinforces limiting beliefs about oneself and others. The Enneagram is designed to promote self-awareness, not to confine people in stereotypes.
- It obstructs empathy and connection: Seeing only someone's Enneagram type can prevent deeper understanding and connection.
- It restricts growth and self-discovery: Using the Enneagram solely for labeling misses the chance to explore deeper personality layers and identify unconscious behavior patterns.

Avoid using the Enneagram as a labeling tool to tap into its full potential for personal growth, empathy, and connection with others.

OVERGENERALIZING ENNEAGRAM STEREOTYPES

Overgeneralizing Enneagram stereotypes can overshadow individual complexities and impede deeper understanding. Stereotyping puts people into rigid boxes which can limit our appreciation of their unique qualities. The Enneagram is a useful self-awareness tool but should not be used to label or categorize.

Each person is a unique blend of traits, motivations, and experiences, shaped by factors such as upbringing, culture, and life experiences. Overgeneralizing stereotypes can reduce people to one-dimensional caricatures, compromising individuality and hindering connection. It's crucial to approach everyone with an open mind, looking beyond any assumptions that may arise from Enneagram stereotypes.

Rather than relying on stereotypes, we should strive for meaningful conversations and genuine connections. Listening and understanding individual perspectives and experiences fosters deeper understanding. Instead of fitting people into a mold, we should appreciate their complexity.

USING ENNEAGRAM TO JUSTIFY BEHAVIOR

Justifying behavior using the Enneagram can limit personal growth and obstruct genuine self-reflection. The Enneagram, a tool for understanding personality types and motivations, shouldn't be used to evade personal accountability or as a rigid behavioral rulebook, but as a framework for self-awareness and growth. Misusing the Enneagram can lead to:

- **Accountability avoidance:** Shifting blame onto our personality type, instead of owning our choices, can inhibit acknowledgment of our flaws and hinder personal development.

- **Personal growth stagnation:** Using our Enneagram type to justify actions can cultivate a fixed mindset, limiting our growth potential and inhibiting self-improvement.
- **Empathy and understanding deficiency:** Utilizing the Enneagram as a behavior excuse can result in a lack of empathy and understanding towards others, leading to dismissal of their feelings or concerns.
- **Authentic self-disconnection:** Justifying behavior with the Enneagram can cause us to lose touch with our authentic selves, as we become overly focused on conforming to our type's mold.

USING ENNEAGRAM TO MANIPULATE OTHERS

When it comes to using the Enneagram to manipulate others, it is important to approach it ethically and responsibly. By understanding the potential for manipulation tactics, you can better recognize when someone may be using the Enneagram to control or influence you. Being aware of these tactics allows you to maintain your autonomy and make informed decisions about how you engage with the Enneagram and those who use it.

Ethical Enneagram Application

Use the Enneagram ethically by avoiding manipulation. It's intended for self-awareness and personal growth, not control or deception. Prioritize empathy, respect for others' autonomy, and fostering genuine connections. Approach it with humility, promote self-reflection, use it for understanding, and respect others' boundaries and choices. The Enneagram should empower, uplift, and support, not manipulate or control.

Recognizing Manipulation Tactics

Beware of those misusing the Enneagram to manipulate others, employing deceitful strategies for control. It's vital to identify these tactics if you aim to help others. Manipulators might exploit the Enneagram to prey on vulnerabilities and dominate others, twisting its teachings for personal gain. They may use guilt, fear, shame, or gaslighting to manipulate and control you. The Enneagram is intended for self-awareness and personal growth, not manipulation. Stay alert and safeguard yourself from its misuse.

IGNORING INDIVIDUAL COMPLEXITY WITH ENNEAGRAM

Don't fall into the trap of simplifying personality types and neglecting personal growth when using the Enneagram. It's important to remember that individuals are complex and multidimensional, and reducing them to a single type can hinder their development. Instead, use the Enneagram as a tool to understand and appreciate the unique complexities and potential for growth in each person.

Simplifying Personality Types

Using the Enneagram for simplifying personality types can overlook individual complexity. It's essential to appreciate each person's uniqueness beyond their single personality type. Here are four potential issues with using Enneagram for simplification:

- Oversimplification: This approach may ignore the unique nuances and intricacies that define an individual.
- Missed Potential: Sole focus on a person's Enneagram type can restrict their growth and potential, disregarding their ability to change and develop.
- Stereotyping: Assigning Enneagram types can foster stereotypes and biases, leading to inaccurate generalizations about their true personality or abilities.
- Lack of Individuality: Neglecting individual complexity can obstruct our capacity to truly understand others, hindering genuine connections.

To truly serve others, it's vital to respect and acknowledge the unique complexities of each person, beyond their Enneagram type.

Neglecting Personal Growth

Ignoring personal growth and the individuality within the Enneagram obscures self-development potential. The Enneagram is a potent tool for self-discovery but isn't universally applicable. Each person's unique experiences, strengths, and challenges must be considered. Ignoring personal growth hinders understanding of self and others. The Enneagram guides towards self-awareness and transformation, but active engagement and facing limitations are essential. Embracing your journey's complexity and committing to personal growth allows the Enneagram's potential to be harnessed for serving others and making a significant impact.

USING ENNEAGRAM TO COMPARE AND COMPETE

Don't misuse the Enneagram to compete or compare negatively. It's a tool for self-discovery and personal growth, not for ego-driven contests or superiority. It should enhance understanding, compassion, empathy, and service to others. To prevent unhealthy competition and comparison, remember:

- **Value individuality:** Each Enneagram type has unique strengths and weaknesses. Focus on understanding and accepting your own, rather than comparing to others.
- **Adopt a growth mindset:** Use the Enneagram for growth and self-improvement, not competition. Learn from others' experiences and see their growth as motivation.
- **Promote empathy and compassion:** Use the Enneagram to understand others' motivations and challenges, fostering connection over competition.

- **Collaborate and learn:** Have open conversations with others using the Enneagram. Share insights, ask questions, and learn together, instead of competing.

Approach the Enneagram with humility, empathy, and a service-oriented mindset to benefit from its transformative power.

USING ENNEAGRAM TO AVOID PERSONAL RESPONSIBILITY

Don't fall into the trap of using the Enneagram as a way to blame others for your actions. It's easy to point fingers and shift responsibility, but that won't lead to personal growth. Instead, take ownership of your choices and use the Enneagram as a tool for self-reflection and development.

Blaming Others for Actions

Using the Enneagram entails taking responsibility for your actions, not blaming others for your decisions. This tool aids in self-awareness and personal growth, but shouldn't be misused to deflect blame. It should enhance your self-understanding, empathy, and compassion. Blaming others is detrimental to personal development. To prevent this:

- Recognize your part in events
- Examine your behaviors and motivations
- Own up to and learn from your mistakes

- Communicate transparently and honestly, aiming for resolution over blame

Ignoring Personal Growth

The Enneagram, while a powerful tool for self-awareness and personal development, should not be used to dodge personal responsibility. It's easy to blame your personality type for your actions, but real growth comes from owning your choices and behaviors. The Enneagram should guide you to better understand yourself and others, not free you from responsibilities. Embrace personal growth and use the Enneagram positively.

Avoiding Self-Reflection

While the Enneagram offers insight into personal behavior and motivations, it shouldn't be used to dodge personal responsibility. It serves as a tool for self-understanding and improving relationships, but sidestepping accountability can hamper progress and potential. Embrace these principles:

- **Accountability:** Don't use the Enneagram to shift blame.
- **Self-reflection:** Use it for honest exploration of thoughts, feelings, and behaviors.
- **Action:** Understanding oneself is the first step; responsibility requires action.
- **Support:** Seek guidance from a mentor or coach for responsible use of the Enneagram.

USING ENNEAGRAM AS A SUBSTITUTE FOR THERAPY

While the Enneagram is a useful tool for self-discovery, it can't replace therapy for tackling deep-seated emotional issues and trauma. Therapy, led by trained professionals, can help uncover the root causes of struggles and provide tools for overcoming them, which the Enneagram cannot offer. Therapy also facilitates a deeper exploration of emotions and experiences, fostering greater self-awareness and self-compassion. Thus, the Enneagram should complement therapy, not replace it. Combining insights from the Enneagram with therapist guidance can boost personal growth and emotional health. Remember, therapy is not a sign of weakness but a brave step towards self-improvement and healing. Recognize the limitations of the Enneagram and seek a qualified therapist's aid for personal growth and emotional well-being.

USING ENNEAGRAM AS A QUICK FIX SOLUTION

While the Enneagram provides useful insights into personality and behavior, it shouldn't be used as a quick fix due to its limitations. It isn't a substitute for professional therapy, especially for deep-rooted emotional or mental health issues. Moreover, it only offers a surface-level understanding of complex personalities, and merely identifying your Enneagram type doesn't provide a complete picture of your individuality. The Enneagram also lacks individualization, as people may exhibit variations of their type, so relying solely on it could overlook personal nuances. Furthermore, self-awareness provided by the Enneagram isn't enough; taking action, like seeking support and practicing self-care, is crucial for growth. Despite the Enneagram's value in personal growth, it requires a realistic approach, understanding that true transformation involves time, effort, and a comprehensive method.

NEGLECTING THE SPIRITUAL ASPECT OF ENNEAGRAM

Ignoring the spiritual component of the Enneagram can limit its potential for transformation. A mere focus on its psychological aspects overlooks its deeper, holistic nature embracing the mind, body, and soul. By not considering its spiritual side, you lose a chance to connect with your higher self and gain inner wisdom. The Enneagram is a pathway to self-discovery and growth, with spirituality as a key player. Overlooking this hinders your understanding of yourself and others.

Spirituality helps transcend ego, access higher consciousness, and foster compassion, empathy, and forgiveness. With a spiritual approach, the Enneagram becomes a tool for self-transformation and spiritual awakening. It also aids in aligning actions and intentions with a higher purpose, encouraging the examination of values, beliefs, and motivations for greater good. Ignoring this aspect risks losing the essence and potential of the Enneagram.

In short, incorporating spirituality in exploring the Enneagram is vital for its transformative power. It facilitates a deeper level of self-awareness, compassion, and purpose. It's important not to neglect this crucial aspect, but to embrace the spiritual journey the Enneagram offers for a meaningful life serving others.

FREQUENTLY ASKED QUESTIONS

Can the Enneagram Accurately Predict Someone's Behavior in All Situations?

Sure, the Enneagram can give you a peek into how you might behave, but it doesn't have all the answers. Think of it as a handy tool for getting to know yourself better, understanding what drives you and how you tend to act. But remember, we're all complex beings. Different things can make us tick at different times. So, use the Enneagram as a starting line, not the finish line. Keep an open mind and use it as a springboard for self-exploration. You've got this!

Is It Possible to Use the Enneagram as a Way to Manipulate or Control Others?

Can you use the Enneagram to control or manipulate others? Let's cut to the chase. Although the Enneagram can offer useful insights into how people behave, it's not for controlling or manipulating anyone. It's important to keep in mind that the Enneagram is a tool for self-improvement and personal growth, not a means to take advantage of or control others. Always interact with people with respect and empathy, no matter what their Enneagram type is.

Can the Enneagram Be Used as a Substitute for Therapy?

Thinking of swapping therapy for the Enneagram? Hold on a minute. Sure, the Enneagram can give you great insights into your personality and behavior, but it's not a substitute for a trained therapist's guidance and support. Therapy provides a safe place to delve into your deeper feelings and traumas - something the Enneagram might not cover completely. So, consider using the Enneagram as a helpful addition to therapy, not as a total replacement. You've got this!

Is It Fair to Compare and Compete With Others Based on Their Enneagram Type?

Should you match yourself up against others based on their Enneagram type? It's like trying to squeeze a square block into a round hole. Everyone is special, with their own set of pros and cons. Rather than turning it into a competition, why not celebrate our differences and learn from each other? The Enneagram is a guide to self-understanding, not a tool for measuring up. Use it to get to know yourself better and build empathy for others.

Is the Enneagram Solely Focused on Personality Traits, or Does It Also Consider Spiritual Aspects?

The Enneagram is more than just a tool to understand your personality - it dives into your spiritual side too. It helps you figure out what motivates you and what you truly want, guiding you towards personal and spiritual growth. By learning about your Enneagram type, you can uncover your unique strengths and challenges. This can help you build a stronger relationship with yourself and those around you. Just remember to keep an open mind and heart while using the Enneagram. It's a tool for self-discovery and fostering understanding and compassion for others.

CONCLUSION

Let's wrap up this chapter with a word of caution: tread carefully with the enneagram. Sure, it provides some pretty interesting insights into different personality types. However, if we misuse it, we might end up with misunderstandings, wrongful labeling, sweeping overgeneralizations, and even manipulation. It's not a free pass for bad behavior or a stand-in for professional therapy. Ignoring its spiritual side and hoping for instant solutions may stunt your personal development. But, if you approach the enneagram with responsibility, it can be a powerful tool for self-discovery and growth.

CHAPTER 19
OTHER BOOKS, PODCASTS, RESOURCES

This chapter is your guide to a treasure trove of bespoke resources meant just for your distinct personality type. Interested? We've hand-picked books, podcasts, and resources that will equip you to blossom, aid others, and unlock your fullest potential. Regardless of your type, you're about to embark on an exciting voyage of self-realization and personal growth. Ready to take the plunge? Let's get started!

ENNEAGRAM TYPE 1 RESOURCES

Enneagram Type 1s seeking personal growth can utilize several resources. Your desire to serve others and have a positive impact can be supported by these recommendations.

Books: 1. 'The Road Back to You' by Ian Morgan Cron and Suzanne Stabile dives deep into each Enneagram type, including Type 1, offering practical guidance for personal growth. 2. 'The Wisdom of the Enneagram' by Don Richard Riso and Russ Hudson provides a comprehensive analysis of each Enneagram type's motivations and behaviors.

Podcasts: 1. 'The Enneagram Journey' with Suzanne Stabile features interviews with Enneagram experts and individuals, including Type 1s, providing valuable insights. 2. 'Typology' with Ian Morgan Cron explores the Enneagram and your Type 1 personality's impact on relationships and personal growth through interviews.

Online Communities: 1. The Enneagram Institute offers a trove of resources, articles, workshops, and forums to connect with other Type 1s. 2. The Enneagram Global Summit allows you to access workshops and presentations from Enneagram experts for personal growth.

ENNEAGRAM TYPE 2 RECOMMENDATIONS

Enneagram Type 2s can enhance personal growth by using resources that align with their caring and empathetic traits. Type 2s often overlook their own needs in favor of others, making it essential to focus on self-care and set healthy boundaries. Here are some helpful recommendations:

1. 'The Road Back to You' by Ian Morgan Cron and Suzanne Stabile provides insights into the Enneagram system, aiding in self-discovery and understanding personal motivations.

2. Brené Brown's 'The Gifts of Imperfection' delves into the significance of vulnerability and self-compassion, advocating for acceptance of flaws and reducing the need for external validation.

3. Suzanne Stabile's 'The Enneagram Journey' podcast offers expert insights and advice for personal growth and self-awareness through interviews and discussions.

4. Mindfulness and meditation practices can enhance presence and self-awareness, providing the clarity needed to focus on self-care.

For Type 2s, it's crucial to balance serving others with self-care, and these resources can aid in fostering self-understanding, setting boundaries, and maintaining authenticity.

BOOKS, PODCASTS, AND RESOURCES FOR ENNEAGRAM TYPE 3

Looking for resources to better understand yourself as an Enneagram Type 3? Check out these recommended books, podcasts, and resources specifically tailored for your type. Discover the best books that delve into the motivations and behaviors of Type 3s, as well as podcasts that provide insightful discussions and interviews with experts in the field. These resources will help you gain a deeper understanding of yourself and navigate your journey towards personal growth.

Enneagram 3 Resource Recommendations

Here are three key resources for Enneagram Type 3 individuals:

1. 'The Road Back to You' by Ian Morgan Cron and Suzanne Stabile offers a comprehensive guide to each Enneagram type, including Type 3, with a focus on personal development. It aids Type 3s in understanding their motivations, fears and desires, facilitating healthy growth.
2. 'The Enneagram Journey' podcast with Suzanne Stabile delves into the Enneagram system, offering valuable insights for self-discovery. Stabile's expert and compassionate approach makes it an excellent resource for Type 3 individuals pursuing personal growth.
3. The Enneagram Institute website provides a vast array of information tailored to each Enneagram type, including Type 3, to help recognize unhealthy patterns, develop self-awareness, and promote personal growth. It's an invaluable tool for Type 3s seeking to understand themselves and navigate their personal journey.

Best Books for Type 3

Discover top books, podcasts, and resources for Enneagram Type 3 individuals. Enhance your journey towards authenticity with resources such as 'The Road Back to You' by Ian Morgan Cron and Suzanne Stabile, which offers insights into the Enneagram system and Type 3 behavior. Ian Morgan Cron's 'Typology' podcast features interviews with various Enneagram types, offering guidance for Type 3s. The Enneagram Institute website provides tailored resources for Type 3s, including articles, workshops, and online courses to aid in self-awareness, growth, and fulfillment.

Top Podcasts for Type 3

Explore the best podcasts for Type 3 individuals that offer insights and guidance on the Enneagram system and Type 3 behavior. These podcasts aim to enhance your self-understanding and provide tools for personal growth.

1. The Enneagram Journey Podcast: Suzanne Stabile hosts this podcast, exploring the Enneagram spiritually and giving advice to Type 3 individuals to balance their ambition with a sense of purpose.
2. Typology Podcast: Hosted by Ian Morgan Cron, this podcast delves into the Enneagram, offering interviews with experts and stories that Type 3 individuals can relate to. It aids in understanding personal motivations and handling Type 3-specific challenges.
3. The Liturgists Podcast: This podcast, while not entirely Enneagram-focused, discusses a variety of topics from a spiritual standpoint. Episodes about identity, authenticity, and achievement cater to Type 3 individuals pursuing fulfillment beyond success.

These podcasts offer new viewpoints, practical tools, and deeper self-understanding for Type 3 individuals, promoting continuous learning and personal development.

ENNEAGRAM TYPE 4: MUST-READS AND PODCASTS

Enneagram Type 4 individuals can deepen their understanding of emotions and creativity with these resources:

- 'The Wisdom of the Enneagram' by Don Richard Riso and Russ Hudson, a comprehensive guide to the Enneagram system, offering insight into each type, including Type 4, with advice on personal growth and relationships.
- 'The Liturgists Podcast' hosted by Michael Gungor and Mike McHargue, which discusses faith, doubt, science, and art, encouraging deep reflection and emotional exploration.
- 'The Artist's Way' by Julia Cameron, a classic book providing practical exercises to overcome creative blocks and unleash artistic potential.
- 'The RobCast' hosted by Rob Bell, covering spirituality, creativity, and personal growth, resonating with those seeking deep exploration and self-expression.
- 'The Road Back to You' by Ian Morgan Cron and Suzanne Stabile, providing a compassionate insight into Enneagram types, including Type 4,

with advice on self-awareness, relationships, and personal growth.

These resources will offer valuable insights into your emotions, creativity, and personal growth, helping you explore your inner world and use your unique gifts to serve others.

TOP RESOURCES FOR ENNEAGRAM TYPE 5

For Enneagram Type 5 individuals seeking personal growth and knowledge enhancement, these resources are recommended. Type 5s are characterized by their curiosity and desire to comprehend the world, and these resources can help cultivate their intellectual and emotional intelligence.

1. 'The Wisdom of the Enneagram' by Don Richard Riso and Russ Hudson: This book delivers a detailed understanding of the Enneagram system, and insights into Type 5 motivations and behaviors, aiding self-awareness.
2. 'The Power of Now' by Eckhart Tolle: This book emphasizes living in the present and eschewing overthought, which can be helpful for Type 5s who may struggle with staying present.
3. 'The Gift of Being Yourself' by David G. Benner: With a focus on self-acceptance, this book can assist Type 5s in combating self-doubt and criticism, promoting self-compassion and authenticity.

4. 'The Road Back to You' by Ian Morgan Cron and Suzanne Stabile: A practical introduction to the Enneagram, including interviews with each type, offering insights and advice for personal growth.

Podcasts like 'The Enneagram Journey' with Suzanne Stabile and 'The Enneagram Panels Podcast' also provide further understanding of Type 5 and the Enneagram system. Engage with these resources with an open mind and eagerness to learn and grow.

ENNEAGRAM TYPE 6: BOOKS AND PODCASTS TO EXPLORE

Want to understand Enneagram Type 6 better? Here are some suggested books and podcasts:

- **The Wisdom of the Enneagram** by Don Richard Riso and Russ Hudson: A comprehensive guide offering practical insights for personal growth and understanding of each Enneagram type, including Type 6.
- **The Road Back to You: An Enneagram Journey to Self-Discovery** by Ian Morgan Cron and Suzanne Stabile: An engaging book providing valuable insights into Type 6's fears, motivations, and behaviors.
- **Typology Podcast with Ian Morgan Cron**: This podcast features interviews discussing different Enneagram types, including episodes focused on Type 6 for personal development.

- **The Enneagram Journey Podcast with Suzanne Stabile**: Renowned Enneagram teacher Suzanne Stabile investigates the Enneagram system's effect on our lives, including in-depth discussions on Type 6.
- **The Complete Enneagram: 27 Paths to Greater Self-Knowledge** by Beatrice Chestnut: This book explores the Enneagram's subtypes and variations, offering valuable insights into Type 6.

While exploring these resources, keep an open mind for self-discovery. Reflect on how the insights apply to you. By deepening your knowledge of Type 6, you can improve self-awareness and personal growth. Remember, the Enneagram is a tool to understand yourself and others, fostering more compassionate and fulfilling relationships.

RECOMMENDED RESOURCES FOR ENNEAGRAM TYPE 7

Looking for resources to deepen your understanding of Enneagram Type 7? Check out these recommendations for books that explore the motivations and challenges of Type 7s, along with podcasts that offer valuable insights and discussions. Additionally, there are top online resources dedicated to Type 7s, providing tools and guidance for personal growth and self-awareness.

Enneagram Type 7 Books

Discover a range of informative books tailored to the growth and self-understanding of Enneagram Type 7s. These resources aid in better comprehending your personality type and its associated challenges and opportunities. Five suggested books are:

- 'The Enneagram: Understanding Yourself and Others in Your Life' by Helen Palmer
- 'The Enneagram Made Easy: Discover the 9 Types of People' by Renee Baron and Elizabeth Wagele
- 'The Wisdom of the Enneagram: The Complete Guide to Psychological and Spiritual Growth for the Nine Personality Types' by Don Richard Riso and Russ Hudson
- 'The Enneagram of Parenting: The 9 Types of Children and How to Raise Them Successfully' by Elizabeth Wagele
- 'The Path Between Us: An Enneagram Journey to Healthy Relationships' by Suzanne Stabile

These books offer valuable insights and practical advice for personal growth, enabling you to capitalize on your strengths and improve weaknesses. Enjoy your reading and self-discovery journey!

Must-listen Podcasts for Type 7

'The Joyful Type Seven' podcast by The Enneagram Journey is a crucial resource for Enneagram Type 7 individuals. It provides insights and guidance tailored to their needs. Host Suzanne Stabile, an Enneagram expert, addresses unique challenges and growth opportunities for Type 7s in each episode. The podcast assists Type 7s in managing their longing for new experiences and pain avoidance. Using the Enneagram framework, listeners can better understand their motivations and patterns, facilitating personal growth. It's an essential tool for Type 7s aiming for intentional living and balance.

Top Online Resources 7s?

The Enneagram Institute's website is a key online resource for Type 7s, providing information to assist their personal growth. Other resources include: The Enneagram Global Summit, an annual online event with expert insights; "The Wisdom of the Enneagram", a book by Don Richard Riso and Russ Hudson full of guidance; The Enneagram Journey Podcast, hosted by Suzanne Stabile, featuring expert discussions; The Enneagram Panels YouTube Channel, offering videos with various perspectives; and The Enneagram Type 7 Subreddit, an online community for shared experiences and support. These tools can help Type 7s enhance self-awareness and personal growth authentically.

ENNEAGRAM TYPE 8: ESSENTIAL BOOKS AND PODCASTS

As an Enneagram Type 8, certain books and podcasts can enrich your self-understanding and personal growth journey. 'The Wisdom of the Enneagram' by Riso and Hudson provides a detailed overview of each type, including Type 8, and offers practical growth tools. The podcast 'The Enneagram Journey' with Suzanne Stabile explores each type deeply, with specific episodes for Type 8. 'The Sacred Enneagram' by Heuertz offers a spiritual perspective, combining Enneagram with contemplative practices. The 'Typology' podcast with Ian Morgan Cron features interviews with each type, offering practical insights for Type 8s. Engaging with these resources can enhance your Type 8 understanding and equip you to serve others authentically.

HELPFUL RESOURCES FOR ENNEAGRAM TYPE 9

Looking for helpful resources to deepen your understanding of Enneagram Type 9? Check out these book recommendations specifically tailored for Type 9s, which will provide valuable insights and strategies for personal growth. Additionally, explore podcasts that discuss Type 9 characteristics and offer practical advice for navigating challenges. Lastly, don't forget to explore online resources that provide further information and support for Type 9 individuals on their Enneagram journey.

Enneagram 9 Book Recommendations

Several books offer valuable insights and practical strategies for individuals with Enneagram Type 9. Five recommended books are: 'The Wisdom of the Enneagram' by Don Richard Riso and Russ Hudson, 'The Road Back to You: An Enneagram Journey to Self-Discovery' by Ian Morgan Cron and Suzanne Stabile, 'The Enneagram: A Christian Perspective' by Richard Rohr and Andreas

Ebert, 'The Sacred Enneagram: Finding Your Unique Path to Spiritual Growth' by Christopher L. Heuertz, and 'The Complete Enneagram: 27 Paths to Greater Self-Knowledge' by Beatrice Chestnut. These resources offer various perspectives and tools to support personal growth and a fulfilling life for Type 9s.

Podcasts for Type 9s

Explore resources tailored for Enneagram Type 9 through podcasts that align with your desire to serve and harmonize relationships. For instance, 'The Enneagram Journey' with Suzanne Stabile provides insights, stories, and advice on how Type 9s can navigate conflicts, assert needs, and find their voice. This podcast can help you understand yourself better and grow and serve more effectively.

Online Resources for Type 9s

Explore these concise yet comprehensive online resources for Enneagram Type 9s, aiding your personal growth journey:

- **Enneagram Institute**: Provides detailed insights into Type 9's motivations, strengths, and growth areas.
- **Enneagram Worldwide**: Offers webinars and online courses for Type 9s, fostering self-awareness and healthier behavior patterns.
- **The Enneagram Journey Podcast**: A Type 9-hosted podcast sharing valuable insights and practical guidance.

- **9 Types Co**: Provides resources like articles and videos exploring the unique challenges and opportunities for Type 9s in personal and professional sectors.
- **The Wisdom of the Enneagram by Don Richard Riso and Russ Hudson**: A comprehensive Enneagram guidebook with practical growth strategies.

These resources will support your self-discovery and personal growth journey as a Type 9, helping you understand and navigate your personality to live a more authentic life.

ENNEAGRAM TYPE 1: ADDITIONAL READING AND PODCASTS

For Enneagram Type 1 individuals seeking to enhance their understanding, the recommended books 'The Road Back to You' by Ian Morgan Cron and Suzanne Stabile, and 'Personality Types' by Don Richard Riso and Russ Hudson, offer valuable insights into Type 1 and its challenges. Podcasts 'The Enneagram Journey' with Suzanne Stabile and 'Typology' with Ian Morgan Cron also provide comprehensive information on Type 1. These resources aid in self-discovery and personal development, offering practical advice and deep insights into motivations and fears. Immersing in these will help you better understand yourself and others, supporting your journey towards self-improvement.

BOOKS, PODCASTS, AND RESOURCES FOR ENNEAGRAM TYPE 2

Enneagram Type 2 individuals can further their understanding and service skills with several recommended resources. Consider these:

- 'The Enneagram: A Christian Perspective' by Richard Rohr and Andreas Ebert explores the Enneagram from a spiritual perspective, useful for those seeking to merge faith with personal growth.
- 'The Enneagram Journey' podcast, hosted by Suzanne Stabile, provides deep insights into all Enneagram types, including Type 2, offering practical tools for personal growth.
- The Enneagram Institute website (www.enneagraminstitute.com) is a comprehensive online resource offering in-depth type descriptions, growth paths, and development suggestions.
- 'The Wisdom of the Enneagram' by Don Richard Riso and Russ Hudson provides a detailed look at each Enneagram type, including Type 2, and practical self-awareness, growth, and relationship guidance.
- 'Typology' podcast, hosted by Ian Morgan Cron, features interviews offering insights into the personal journeys of various Enneagram types, including Type 2.

Engaging with these resources will deepen your understanding of Type 2 tendencies, reveal blind spots, and provide strategies for personal growth and balanced service to others. Explore these resources to aid your Enneagram journey.

ENNEAGRAM TYPE 3: FURTHER EXPLORATION AND RECOMMENDATIONS

Delve into Enneagram Type 3 with recommended books, podcasts, and resources for personal growth. These tools can aid in navigating the complexities of being a Type 3. 'The Road Back to You' by Ian Morgan Cron and Suzanne Stabile is a recommended book that offers a thorough understanding of each Enneagram type, including practical advice for personal and spiritual growth.

The podcast 'Typology' by Ian Morgan Cron provides valuable insights from interviews with different Enneagram types. The Enneagram Institute's website (www.enneagraminstitute.com) provides detailed information on each Enneagram type, with articles, workshops, and online courses for further development.

Exploring these resources can deepen your understanding of your Type 3 personality and provide practical tools for authentic and purposeful living. Your desire to serve others is a gift, and these resources can help you use it in a meaningful and fulfilling way.

RECOMMENDED RESOURCES FOR ENNEAGRAM TYPE 4

For personal growth and understanding of Enneagram Type 4, consider these five resources:

- **'The Wisdom of the Enneagram'** by Don Richard Riso and Russ Hudson offers deep insights into Type 4 and practical tools for personal growth.
- **The Enneagram Institute** (enneagraminstitute.com) provides articles, podcasts, and workshops specifically for Type 4s seeking self-discovery and development.
- **'The Road Back to You'** by Ian Morgan Cron and Suzanne Stabile offers an accessible introduction to the Enneagram system, including insights into Type 4.
- **The Liturgists Podcast**, hosted by Michael Gungor and Mike McHargue, discusses the Enneagram through spirituality, art, and science, making it an engaging resource for Type 4 individuals.
- **The Narrative Enneagram** (narrativeenneagram.org) provides workshops and resources tailored to each Enneagram type, including a supportive environment for Type 4 individuals to explore emotions, creativity, and relationships.

Use these resources for self-discovery and personal growth, embracing them with an open mind and willingness to delve into your unique personality.

FREQUENTLY ASKED QUESTIONS

Are There Any Resources Specifically Tailored for Enneagram Type 1s Who Are Also Parents or in a Leadership Role?

Are you a parent or a leader and also a type 1 on the Enneagram? You might be looking around for resources designed just for you. Good on you for seeking help and support! Yes, there are resources out there that can help you navigate these roles, understand yourself better, manage your habits, and come up with effective strategies. These resources can really make a difference in your parenting or leadership journey.

Are There Any Enneagram Type 2 Podcasts That Focus on Relationships and Communication?

Are you on the hunt for Enneagram type 2 podcasts that focus on relationships and communication? Good news! There's a wealth of podcasts out there, crafted just for type 2s like you. These podcasts offer valuable advice and insights to help you improve your relationships and communication skills. So, brace yourself for a journey of learning and growth through these custom-made podcasts!

Can You Recommend Any Books or Resources for Enneagram Type 3s Who Are Interested in Personal Development and Goal-Setting?

Are you an Enneagram Type 3 aiming for personal growth and goal setting? Good for you! There are numerous books and tools available that can guide you on this path. Whether you want to boost your leadership abilities or get better at balancing work and life, there's a resource out there for you. So go ahead, start exploring and see how you can unlock your true potential. It's time to thrive!

Are There Any Enneagram Type 4 Books That Delve Into the Creative Process and Artistic Expression?

Are you an Enneagram Type 4 looking to delve into the creative process and artistic expression? There's a wealth of books available that can guide and inspire you on this journey. Whether you're into writing, painting, or making music, these books will help you understand your emotions and find your unique creative voice. They're designed to unlock your full artistic potential. So, get ready to let your creativity flow!

Can You Suggest Any Resources for Enneagram Type 5s Who Are Interested in Deepening Their Understanding of Psychology and Philosophy?

You're a Type 5 and want to dive deeper into psychology and philosophy? You're in luck! There's plenty of stuff out there to help you out. Books, podcasts, you name it. They're all ready to give you a better grip on what you're keen on. You're just a few clicks away from expanding your knowledge and getting fresh insights. So, if it's book suggestions or psychology-themed podcasts you're after, rest assured, you've got plenty of resources to boost your understanding. Dive in!

CONCLUSION

There are heaps of resources out there ready to guide you on your journey to self-discovery and personal growth. Books, podcasts - you name it, it's there. Why not dive in and explore your Enneagram type a little more? Remember the old adage, 'Knowledge is power' (You 5s know what I'm talking about). So, grab that power and continue to learn and grow. Don't just read the chapter, live it!

CHAPTER 20

HOW TO FIND A QUALIFIED ENNEAGRAM COACH

Are you searching for a top-notch Enneagram coach to guide you on your personal growth journey? You're in the right place! In this chapter, we'll walk you through some simple but powerful steps to find the perfect coach for you. Following these tips, you'll soon find an experienced and supportive Enneagram coach who will fuel your journey to reach your maximum potential. Ready to dive in? Let's get started!

RESEARCH ENNEAGRAM COACHING QUALIFICATIONS

To investigate enneagram coaching qualifications, first find resources that detail accredited certifications and training programs. Ensuring proper training and certification is key for credibility and professional development. Programs should cover enneagram system fundamentals, practical application, and provide hands-on experience to develop effective coaching skills.

Consider the experience of the trainers, as their expertise will enhance learning and offer critical insights. Evaluate the support offered by the programs, such as ongoing mentorship, supervision, and a community of fellow coaches.

DETERMINE YOUR COACHING NEEDS AND GOALS

Before seeking an enneagram coach, identify your specific needs and goals. Reflect on your personal and professional life to pinpoint areas needing guidance. Clarifying your goals, such as improving relationships or leadership skills, will help find a suitable coach.

Consider current challenges like communication issues, lack of self-confidence or feeling overwhelmed. Articulating these to potential coaches will allow them to assess their ability to address your concerns.

Establish your coaching goals, such as enhancing self-awareness, emotional intelligence, or life fulfillment. Defining these will help find a coach who aligns with your aspirations and provide a roadmap for your journey.

SEEK RECOMMENDATIONS FROM TRUSTED SOURCES

Seek advice from friends, colleagues, or mentors about reputable enneagram coaches that align with your needs and goals. These individuals, with their personal experiences and insights, can provide valuable recommendations. Be clear about what you're looking for, whether it's career development or personal growth, to receive targeted suggestions. People who have personally benefited from an enneagram coach or professionals in the personal development field can be considered trusted sources for such recommendations. Remember, a qualified enneagram coach should resonate with you, understand your unique needs, and have the expertise to guide you. Using these trusted sources can help you make an informed decision, so don't hesitate to reach out for recommendations on suitable enneagram coaches.

CONDUCT THOROUGH BACKGROUND CHECKS ON POTENTIAL COACHES

When conducting thorough background checks on potential coaches, there are a few key points to consider. Firstly, it is important to verify the coach's credentials and ensure that they have the necessary qualifications and experience in Enneagram coaching. Additionally, seeking client testimonials can provide valuable insights into the coach's effectiveness and the quality of their services. By thoroughly examining these points, you can make an informed decision when choosing an Enneagram coach.

Verify Coach's Credentials

It's crucial to thoroughly check the credentials of potential coaches. Start by researching their educational background, certifications from reputable institutions, and any professional affiliations which reflect their commit-ment to continuous learning. Examine their professional experience and look for positive client testimonials and successful outcomes. Don't shy away from contacting references for further insights. By doing these compre-hensive checks, you can confidently verify the coach's credentials and make an informed decision for your self-development journey.

Seek Client Testimonials

Start your evaluation of potential coaches by seeking client testimonials, which provide insight into their effectiveness, coaching style, and real-world results. These testimonials will help you understand the coach's ability to guide clients on their Enneagram journey. Look for testimonials emphasizing the coach's expertise, empathy, and ability to foster a nurturing space for growth. Check if the clients' outcomes align with your goals. Consider contacting clients directly for more detailed insights. This approach will help you make an informed decision when selecting a coach that aligns with your aspirations.

ASSESS THE COACH'S ENNEAGRAM KNOWLEDGE AND EXPERTISE

To assess a coach's Enneagram knowledge and expertise, consider these three factors:

1. Training and Certification: Ensure the coach has formal Enneagram training and certification

from reputable organizations. This verifies their solid expertise in the Enneagram system.

2. Experience and Practical Application: Choose a coach with proven experience using the Enneagram system and a history of successfully assisting clients with their Enneagram types.

3. Ongoing Learning and Growth: A competent coach should be committed to continuous learning about the evolving Enneagram system. Look for those who frequently attend relevant professional events to stay updated.

EVALUATE THE COACH'S COACHING STYLE AND APPROACH

Evaluate the coach's style and approach by observing their client interactions and ability to foster a supportive and empowering environment. Note whether they listen actively to clients' concerns, ask insightful questions, establish rapport, and create a safe exploration space.

A competent coach encourages clients to take charge of their growth, provides constructive feedback without judgment, and respects their autonomy.

Consider the coach's approach, which could be structured and goal-oriented or intuitive and holistic. Choose an approach that aligns with your growth objectives.

Finding the right coach is a personal choice, requiring research and interaction with potential coaches. Trust your instincts and choose a coach with the right knowledge and expertise, who can support, empower, and inspire you on your Enneagram journey.

SCHEDULE A CONSULTATION SESSION WITH POTENTIAL COACHES

When it comes to finding a qualified Enneagram coach, scheduling a consultation session is crucial. This session allows you to experience the benefits of coaching first-hand and assess the compatibility between you and the potential coach. By engaging in a conversation and asking specific questions, you can gain valuable insights into their coaching style and approach, helping you make an informed decision.

Coaching Session Benefits

Consult with potential coaches to enjoy the advantages of coaching sessions. These sessions offer valuable insights and guidance to better serve others. The three main benefits include:

1. Clarity: Coaches enable you to understand your goals, values, and purpose by asking probing questions and providing a secure environment for exploration.
2. Accountability: Coaches ensure you remain committed to your goals by identifying potential hindrances and creating strategies to overcome them, keeping you focused and motivated.
3. Growth: Coaching sessions foster personal and professional development. Coaches identify

improvement areas and provide tools to enhance skills and abilities, helping you grow and reach your full potential.

Don't miss these benefits. Schedule a consultation with a potential coach today to start your growth journey.

Coach Compatibility Assessment

To ensure a potential coach aligns with your needs, organize a consultation session. This will enable you to evaluate their coaching style, approach, and personality, and for them to understand your unique needs. This process will help determine if you're comfortable with the coach and if they can help achieve your Enneagram goals. Taking the time to do this is vital for your personal growth, so don't rush the decision.

TRUST YOUR INTUITION AND MAKE A FINAL DECISION

Choose the Enneagram coach that aligns with your intuition. This is key in your decision-making process. After researching and assessing potential coaches, listen to your inner voice to find the best fit. Here are three steps to guide you:

1. Reflect on your first interaction: Recall your initial meeting with each coach. Consider any immediate connections or trust you felt, as this could indicate compatibility.

2. Evaluate your emotional reactions: Reflect on your feelings when imagining working with each coach. Do emotions of excitement, inspiration, or comfort arise? These can guide you to a suitable coach.

3. Listen to your intuition: Connect with your inner wisdom. Visualize working with each coach and note which image feels most authentic and aligned. Trust your intuition to lead you to the right coach.

FREQUENTLY ASKED QUESTIONS

How Much Does Enneagram Coaching Typically Cost?

The cost of Enneagram coaching can change based on things like the coach's experience, their training, and where they're located. Usually, you're looking at anywhere from $75 to $200 for each session. But don't forget, while the price matters, picking a well-qualified coach is the most important. Try to find a certified coach with a lot of experience and positive reviews. Don't be shy about asking questions and talking about your goals to make sure you're a good match. After all, you can't put a price on investing in yourself!

Are There Any Certifications or Licenses Required to Become an Enneagram Coach?

So, you're looking for an Enneagram coach? Great choice! Now, there's no official governing body for this type of coaching, but you should still focus on finding a coach with certifications. Not just any certifications, though. Look for those from respected organizations like the International Enneagram Association or the Enneagram Institute. These show a coach's dedication to their profession. Top-notch coaches will have finished intense training programs and really know the ins and outs of the Enneagram system. Trust your gut when picking a coach. If they feel right to you personally, they probably are. Stay motivated and you'll find the right coach in no time!

Can Enneagram Coaching Be Done Remotely or Is It Typically Done in Person?

Sure, you can do Enneagram coaching either remotely or face-to-face. It all boils down to your preference and the coaches available nearby. With remote coaching, you enjoy flexibility as you can have your sessions through video calls or phone. On the other hand, face-to-face coaching brings a personal touch and interactivity. Think about what suits you best. Feel free to connect with professional coaches to know more and explore your choices.

How Long Does Enneagram Coaching Usually Last?

So, you're curious about how long Enneagram coaching takes, right? Well, it usually spans a few months, but honestly, it depends on what you're looking to achieve. The key is to find a coach who knows the Enneagram inside out and has a track record of helping people like you. Make sure they're certified and well-recommended. Don't shy away from asking them about their coaching style and the kind of support they offer. Remember, the right coach is crucial to make your Enneagram coaching journey a success. You've got this!

Are There Any Specific Ethics or Guidelines That Enneagram Coaches Must Follow?

Looking for a good Enneagram coach? It's crucial they stick to certain ethics and guidelines. These rules help the coach keep their professionalism and honesty in check. What should they do? Keep your secrets safe, respect your space, and guide you without any bias. If your coach follows these, you're in good hands. They'll give you the help and advice you need on your Enneagram journey. You can trust them!

CONCLUSION

Looking for a skilled Enneagram coach? Well, you're on the right track! You've done your homework, asked around, and done some serious vetting. You've judged their expertise and their coaching approach, and even sat down for a chat with them. Now, it's time to trust your gut. It's the inner compass that's leading you. Make the final call and get ready to start an exciting journey with your chosen Enneagram coach. Picture them like a river guide, steering you through the twists and turns, helping you dive deep into self-exploration and personal growth. Have faith in the process and get ready for a transformation.

CHAPTER 21
FINAL THOUGHTS

We did it! We've reached the final stop on our journey of self-discovery and relationship building using the Enneagram. What an absolutely incredible ride it's been!

I hope you feel as pumped and inspired as I do right now after diving deep into the captivating world of the Enneagram. When we started out together, you might have seen the Enneagram as just another personality test to take for fun. But now, I'm betting you can appreciate how much more profound it is than that.

The Enneagram gives us an unparalleled window into the motivations, fears, and desires that drive our behavior. It's like finally getting the decoder ring to understand ourselves and others on a whole new level!

We uncovered the unique characteristics of each of the 9 Enneagram types - yes, those lovely folks we now know as the Perfectionist, the Helper, the Achiever, the Individualist, the Investigator, the Loyalist, the Enthusiast, the Challenger, and the Peacemaker.

It was so eye-opening to realize we don't all see the world the same way. What is vitally important to a Type One Perfectionist like integrity and improvement may mean little to a Type Seven Enthusiast who just wants to live in the moment.

These insights opened the door for so much more compassion, empathy and respect for the differences between us. We're all just walking our own Enneagram path in this life, driven by our core motivations that we may not even be aware of!

Of course, the best part of this journey was figuring out your very own Enneagram type. I hope the self-discovery process shed new light on some of your ingrained patterns, behavior, and emotional reactions. Everything started to click into place when you realized your core desires and fears.

Suddenly, you had an "Aha!" moment that made so much of your life make sense. The Enneagram became your trusted guide to avoid your limitations and maximize your potential. I loved watching your growth as you embraced your Enneagram insights.

Not only that, but your relationships absolutely blossomed when you began interacting with others through the lens of your Enneagram wisdom. It was like you learned the secret Enneagram code to clearly understand those around you for the first time ever!

With your new communication strategies tailored to each type and ability to provide personalized support, your connections grew deeper than you thought possible. It warmed my heart to see you forging such meaningful, fulfilling bonds.

I hope this book has opened a doorway to a lifetime of self-discovery and ever-evolving relationships. Remember, learning about the Enneagram isn't meant to box you into one static category. We are all complex and wondrous beings!

Use the Enneagram as your guide, but don't ever let it limit you. Keep growing beyond the comfort of your type's familiar patterns. Never stop stretching yourself.

You now have the tools to understand the diverse individuals you interact with in your life. But make sure to stay curious and open-minded when encountering people different from you.

The Enneagram is an incredible starting point, but it is not the be-all and end-all. There is always more to learn about yourself and others. Treat it as a stepping stone to deeper wisdom, not an end goal.

As you continue on your journey long after these pages, remember to treat the Enneagram with respect and care. Use it to empower, not limit or manipulate. Share it as a gift, not a weapon.

Approach it with humility, compassion, and ethics at the front of your mind. When shared in the right spirit, it can change lives. But in the wrong hands, it has the capacity to do harm. Stay vigilant!

My dear friend, we have walked many miles together, and I have treasured every step along the way with you. I can't wait to see how you will continue growing and spreading your Enneagram knowledge far and wide.

Never forget, our true purpose in this life is to leave every heart a little more whole than we found it. Armed with the Enneagram, you now have endless opportunities to make a meaningful difference in people's lives.

So go forth with courage and make your unique mark on this world! Thank you for letting me be a small part of your incredible journey.

ABOUT THE
AUTHOR

Kim Pryor Jones is an expert in emotional regulation, marriage counseling, and the Enneagram. With decades of experience in the field of personal development and psychology, she has helped countless individuals understand and manage their emotions. As a writer, she is passionate about sharing her knowledge and empowering others to take control of their emotional wellbeing.

Her book, Understanding Emotional Regulation for Adults, provides practical tools and strategies for managing difficult emotions and building resilience. Kim's compassionate approach and deep understanding of the human psyche make her a trusted guide for anyone seeking to improve their emotional health.

You can read more of her Enneagram work at:

https://theenneagramtypes.com